Best wishes to Margaret and Jimmy,

James Moir

Travels
in the
Holy Land

Travels in the Holy Land

James Martin

LOCHAR PUBLISHING • MOFFAT • SCOTLAND

© James Martin, 1991
Published by Lochar Publishing
MOFFAT DG10 9ED

British Library Cataloguing in Publication Data

Martin, James, 1921-
Travels in the Holy Land.
I. Title
915.6940454

ISBN-0-948403-82-9

Printed in Great Britain by BPCC Wheatons Ltd, Exeter

This book is dedicated to all who have gone on pilgrimage with me to the Holy Land, especially my wife, Marion, and those like her who have given enormous help to my leadership as burden-bearers, as counsellors and in other ways.

After this book was written and as it was being prepared for publication, the whole of the Middle East, including the Holy Land, was thrown into turmoil with the outbreak of hostilities in the Gulf. Over the years I have made many friends in the Holy Land, with people of different races and different creeds. As a result the present situation carries for me all the greater poignancy and concern. My earnest prayer is that very soon - even, I hope, before this book appears - the warfare will have ceased and that peace, real peace, will have taken its place.

Contents

Introduction

$\mathbf{A}$s a leader of Christian pilgrimages to the Holy Land for the past quarter of a century, I have been asked many times, 'Do you not find it a bit dull, even boring, going over the same ground time after time, year after year? Surely it must have become a very monotonous chore?'

I never need any time to reflect on my answer. It is always an emphatic, 'No'. I never find it dull, far less boring, and I cannot imagine that I ever will. Apart from the sheer exhilaration and inspiration of 'walking where Jesus walked', each trip has its own distinctive character and flavour. This is due not only and not even chiefly to the fact that, while for obvious reasons the basic itinerary must remain the same, in every pilgrimage I try to introduce some variety into its minor components. Much more is it due to the fact that each and every pilgrimage has its own unique incidents and encounters. In addition, each group of pilgrims has its own measure of distinctiveness; it is a rare group that does not include some 'characters' who for one reason or another help to make the tour a memorable one.

This book is an attempt to convey something of the thrill and atmosphere as well as the enjoyment of a visit to the Holy Land by relating not simply the places to be seen but also the people and some of the happenings that were part of the tours I have been privileged to lead.

The Outward Journey

Even in these world-shortened modern days, for all but the most blasé of travellers, journeying to a foreign land can still be an enthralling experience. For anyone with religious faith, travelling to the Holy Land is likely to be particularly so, especially if it is for the first time. Many 'first-time' pilgrims are very much aware that, for financial or other reasons, their first time is likely to be their only time; and this awareness serves to intensify the feeling of excitement at embarking upon what has often been referred to as 'the journey of a lifetime'.

Obviously this journey has to begin somewhere, and for my Holy Land pilgrimages, the departure point is usually Heathrow Airport. But getting to the departure point may often carry its own measure of excitement - leaving home and making one's way by air, road or rail from various points in the United Kingdom or further afield.

Even this preliminary stage - before the tour proper has begun - can contain potential anxiety or difficulty for the group leader.

On one occasion I was sitting comfortably and contentedly in an aisle seat of the aircraft winging its way on time and in good weather from Glasgow to Heathrow. I was contented because my Glasgow contingent had turned up punctually and were all now safely aboard, soon to rendezvous with the rest of my group at Heathrow before boarding the plane for Israel.

Directly across the passage from me sat John Sergeant. He had been with me to the Holy Land before and I knew him to be the most methodical of men. He never forgot anything, never mislaid anything, never slipped up on any item of pre-tour preparation. His daughter, Patricia, who was making the trip for the first time, was completely different - slapdash, inattentive to detail, and frequently ill-organised. John, I well knew, would have had to organise Pat's preparations, and even her packing, as well as his own.

That, I imagine, was the reason and the explanation for the thunderbolt he

Travels in the Holy Land

was about to toss into my lap.

Suddenly he leaned across to me and said in a very quiet voice - so quiet that the full import of his words took fully a second to penetrate my consciousness - 'Mr Martin, I've left my passport behind'.

'Don't make jokes like that, John,' I said, knowing so well that John Sergeant of all people could never commit the cardinal overseas traveller's sin of omitting to bring his passport, 'It's not good for my blood pressure'.

'It's not a joke', he continued in the same quiet voice, 'I laid it down on the sideboard intending to put it in my pocket before we went to the car and I've left it there'.

My heart sank. There was simply no way, I knew, that John would be permitted to fly out to Israel without his passport but the problem was how could he possibly get hold of that passport before we were due to embark.

The only hope lay in the fact that a neighbour held a set of John's house keys. If he could be contacted to pick up the passport and have it sent down on the next Glasgow/Heathrow flight all might still be well. The cabin crew were immensely considerate and helpful. The story was radioed back to Glasgow and the appropriate wheels were set in motion.

Our hopes ran high but were dashed when, on arrival at Heathrow, we were informed that the neighbour was away from home for the day. After some to-ing and fro-ing, and an abortive attempt to obtain a temporary passport that would be acceptable for entry into Israel, we had to accept the fact that John Sergeant would not be flying out to Israel that day.

By now time had run out on me. I could no longer delay taking my group through passport and security control preparatory to boarding the aircraft for Tel Aviv. I had, of course, to leave John behind and Pat elected to stay with him. My concern for their plight was soon mitigated by the concern and attention of the British Airways staff.

'Don't worry about them', they assured me, 'We'll have the passport down from Glasgow in plenty of time for them to fly out with us tomorrow'. All the same, it was not without some concern that I took to the air with two of my group still on the ground. However, John and Pat did meet up with us in Jerusalem the following day. But they were six hours later than expected and John could hardly wait to tell us his tale.

Once the missing passport had duly arrived, the stewardess of our Glasgow/London flight, who had already been extremely helpful, took John and Pat to her London flat where they spent the night. The next morning, clutching his passport, John checked in along with Pat in good time for the flight to Israel. They found to their surprise and delight that they were given seats in the first class cabin as the rest of the aircraft was full, and proceeded to enjoy the additional comfort thus provided in a flight which departed right on time.

The Outward Journey

The traumas of the previous day were all but forgotten and even the loss of a touring day had ceased to bother them when, suddenly, halfway to Tel Aviv, the captain announced that they were required to turn round and head back to Heathrow. A hiccup of some kind had developed at Ben Gurion Airport which necessitated its closure for a period. Since there was no guarantee of their being able to land on arrival some two and a quarter hours ahead, there was no alternative but to go back to Heathrow. By the time of touchdown at Heathrow, the difficulty at Ben Gurion was over and the airport was again open to traffic. So, after refuelling, the aircraft took off once more and this time deposited our laggard fellow-travellers in Ben Gurion where our travel agent met them and whisked them to our hotel in Jerusalem to rejoin us there.

That has been the only occasion when I have departed from Heathrow without having all my party with me. But there have been a few occasions when I have had a headache wondering whether or not they were all going to make it.

There were Ruby and Iris, for instance, who were travelling to London by rail and whose train was due to arrive with oodles of time to spare. But a serious accident closed their line completely and their train had to be so drastically re-routed that they reached Heathrow long after they were due to check in and very shortly indeed before take-off time.

We were flying EL-AL which is surely the most security-conscious airline in the world. Because of this, late arrival for a flight can easily jeopardise one's prospects of being allowed to claim one's seat. Ruby and Iris were not only late, they were very late. As I waited in the departure lounge with the rest of the group, with all our pre-flight formalities completed and expecting the boarding call very soon, I was reconciled to having to depart without them. Then, to my great relief, they arrived. An explanation of the circumstances which had led to their late arrival, coupled perhaps with their ingenuous charm, had been enough to overcome the obstacles.

It was charm, I am sure, which did the trick for Alasdair when he turned up rather late. I had never previously met him but, in addition to considerable correspondence, I had had a number of telephone conversations with him to his north of Scotland home. In the course of these, as I did with everyone, I had impressed on him the necessity of being at the check-in desk not later than 1.30 pm so that we might all pass through the various formalities two and a half hours before the departure time of 4.15 pm as we were required to do.

Everyone was there at 1.30 except Alasdair and when 2 pm came and there was still no sign of him, I had to take my group through, despite my anxiety about his non-arrival. As 3 pm approached, that anxiety increased tenfold as I began to wonder what disaster must have overtaken our absent friend. But at 2.55 Alasdair sauntered nonchalantly along and, being the very last passenger to present himself, passed through all the formalities much more quickly and much more easily than any of the hundreds who had preceded him.

'I'm so relieved to see you', I said when he joined us, 'Did you have difficulty getting here?'

'None at all', he replied in his soft highland drawl, 'I had no trouble at all.'

'Oh,' I said, somewhat nonplussed, 'perhaps I didn't make it plain that everyone was to meet at one o'clock.'

'You made it plain enough', Alasdair came back, 'But when I thought about it, I felt sure that I didn't need to be here anything like so early.'

Another who turned up worryingly late was Ivy. Our little Glasgow contingent had arrived at Heathrow in good time and made its way to the EL-AL desk to collect our boarding passes from the Inter-Church Travel representative, before going through the first stage of passport and security control en route to the departure lounge. The representative managed to single me out instantly as the clergyman who was leading the tour - perhaps aided slightly by the fact that I was the only member of the group wearing a clerical collar and a badge with my name clearly printed on it. Brightly he said to me, 'I've got both good news and bad news for you. Which do you want to hear first?'

'I'd better have the bad news first', I replied.

'The bad news is that your flight departure has been delayed five hours. The good news is that those of your group who have arrived at Heathrow are being taken to a hotel where they will all be allocated rooms and be given lunch. The rest of the group live close enough for us to have contacted them and advised them to report five hours later than the original time.'

The flight delay was a blow and I immediately began to fret as to how I could possibly get the next morning's touring schedule started even approximately on time when we were now definitely not going to reach our Jerusalem hotel before dawn.

The hotel rooms, however, were pleasant, and so was the lunch. When in due course we received the summons to board the hotel's courtesy coach and head for the airport terminal, I heaved a great sign of relief. Very soon now, I thought, I will be able to relax. But I did not then know about Ivy.

Ivy was from London and one of those whom the company had been able to advise not to come to the airport until the later time. Ivy, it seemed, interpreted the 'later' instruction rather more liberally than the others. She arrived considerably later, so much later that all the rest of us had long been checked in right through to the EL-AL departure lounge. As we were waiting there for the announcement that would call us to board, the man in charge of the security checking came and took me away for consultation about a problem. The problem was Ivy.

Checking in a group for the EL-AL flight from Heathrow to Ben Gurion (Tel Aviv) is a very disciplined, if often rather tedious, process. After being issued with our boarding passes by our representative, we file through passport control and the first (British) security check which involves a thorough examination of all our baggage. This admits us to the overseas departure lounge. The next stage is to take ourselves and our baggage to the somewhat distant Gate 23 where we face the EL-AL security screening of individuals and their luggage. Only then are we able to have our heavy baggage despatched towards the aircraft hold.

It was after my group and practically every other intending traveller had arrived at this point that I was called out by the security officer. 'We have a problem that concerns you', he said, 'with a lady who claims to be one of your group'. When he mentioned Ivy's name, I was able to confirm that she was indeed one of my group. 'Well', he went on, 'we have a problem concerning her. Please come with me.'

Full of foreboding, I followed him to meet Ivy, who was in an understandably agitated state. The problem was not her late arrival. That was the least of it. The problem was that she could not produce a boarding pass. The fact that she was in that area without one was naturally viewed with grave suspicion by the security staff. What is more, of course, without a boarding pass there was no way she would be allowed to board the plane.

It seemed utterly beyond belief that Ivy could have got as far as she had without being able to produce a boarding pass at the earlier checkpoints, despite her insistence that she had not been given one by the tour representative who had waited to attend to the later arrivals. It seemed much more likely that she had somehow lost her boarding pass in making her way from the first check-in point to the second. Either way the situation was serious.

The security supervisor reiterated several times that it was out of the question for Ivy to be permitted to board the aircraft unless she could produce her boarding pass. The computer made it plain that the pass had been issued and it was not permissible to issue a duplicate without having established the fate of the original. He postulated all the sinister possibilities: the lady standing before us could be, for instance, an infiltrator to the scheduled passenger complement with evil intent - and I, not having set eyes on her until half an hour previously, was in no position to testify that she was the Ivy who was listed among the passengers.

We had virtually abandoned all hope of getting Ivy on the flight when, quite suddenly, his attitude seemed to soften. Whether it was because of my continued pleas - for I had no doubt that she was indeed the lady we were waiting for to complete our group - or because of some word from on high through his walkie-talkie, I cannot tell. All I know is that I did not stop to argue, far less demur, when he said that if I accepted full responsibility he would issue a duplicate boarding pass to Ivy. This he did; but if I thought that all my worries concerning Ivy would now be over I had assuredly another think coming.

Once the tour was begun, it soon emerged that Ivy slept only little and fitfully, and in her waking hours through the night she liked to rise and stroll around the bedroom singing hymns in a fairly loud voice. After two nights of this the lady with whom she shared a room felt she had come to the end of her physical tether. I was left with no option but to go cap in hand to the hotel management and beg an additional room, never an easy thing to obtain in the busy season.

Then I had to be surety for Ivy again, this time regarding a financial matter. We discovered that none of the traveller's cheques in her possession had been signed so that, as a result, she was virtually penniless in a foreign land. When she telephoned home, her daughter at once arranged for money to be transmitted to her but I had to subsidise her until it arrived.

So far as Ivy was concerned that pilgrimage had a very inauspicious start. In the early stages, I fear, she was beginning to wish she had never come and I was beginning to wonder if it might not have been better for me, too, if after all she had not been permitted to board the plane. But in the end she had a very happy time.

On one never to be forgotten occasion it was the suitcase of one of my party that failed to get on to the plane. Lily was from Ireland and was joining up with me at Heathrow; but she arrived with only her hand luggage and no suitcase. It had not come off the aircraft that had brought her from Belfast; and try as we might we were unable to locate it before it was time to embark for Tel Aviv.

So Lily had to travel out to the Holy Land with only the very few items she was carrying in her hand luggage. British Airways assured us, however, that as soon as the suitcase was located it would be sent out and delivered to our Jerusalem hotel. They confidently expected this to be no later than the following day.

But the suitcase did not reach us the following day. Nor the next. Nor the next again. Every day I was on the telephone to the British Airways office at Ben Gurion in an attempt to speed up the discovery and delivery of Lily's missing suitcase. We were all concerned for her. She was lent items of clothing from this person and from that; and she washed her 'smalls' each night, hanging them out on her verandah and finding them completely dry by the morning.

The Outward Journey

All of this Lily accepted with the best of good humour. She kept insisting that the lack of her suitcase and its contents was not detracting in the slightest from what she continually asserted was a simply marvellous tour. 'If I was to lose my suitcase', she said, 'I could not have chosen a better place to do it. This country is so good for getting things dried that I am hardly missing my other clothes at all.'

It was only after we had completed our eight nights in Jerusalem and moved on to Tiberias that the long lost suitcase finally turned up. It was delivered by British Airways special messenger on our first day there. How delighted everyone was. The return of the lost suitcase produced such rejoicing it could almost be likened to that evoked by the return of the lost son in Jesus' famous parable.

But that was not the end of the story. The very next day another suitcase was delivered to us by British Airways, supposedly Lily's. This one clearly did not belong to her as she was already now in possession of hers. On investigation we found out that the second arrival was, in fact, the property of a gentleman who was no doubt presently engaged rather feverishly, as I had recently been, in making incessant telephone calls to British Airways.

The vast difference was that he was not in Israel but in Bahrain - at least that was the address on his suitcase.

Of course I did what I could to alleviate his distress by once more telephoning British Airways to have them pick up the suitcase and load it on the correct aircraft next time round. Lily, for her part, was overjoyed that her suitcase had now been found, and so were we all.

By this time, however, having taken her several times through her account of her departure from Belfast airport, I had become convinced that the true explanation of her missing suitcase was that she had never checked it in. It was her first experience of flying and I am certain that what happened was this: when she presented her ticket, she somehow managed to leave her suitcase on the floor at the side of the desk, thinking that it was no longer her responsibility and that it would automatically be put on the plane.

Her eight days without her suitcase and its contents was an unwelcome inconvenience but I think it was only through the ingenuity of airport staff and the honesty of Irish people that she ever saw it again. It did not seem to spoil Lily's 'whale of a time' in the least. The inconvenience was something that she treated with regal disdain and I never attempted to explain to her what I believe to be the truth of the matter. Far better, I thought, to leave untarnished for her a story with which to delight many a listener for many a day.

Sometimes, although fortunately not often, we have suffered minor mishaps such as these regarding the outward journey. Sometimes we have had frustrating delays. Mostly we have had slow and elaborate security checks but these, if tedious, serve to give us reassurance about safety. But none of these things diminishes the sheer joy and excitement experienced in the anticipation of visiting the Holy Land, whether it be for the first time or a subsequent time - and whatever one's age.

I once acted as chaplain to several hundred schoolchildren on an educational cruise which included two days in the Holy Land. I well remember one young lad saying to me early on, practically at the beginning of the outward journey, 'I'm so excited about this trip'.

'What makes you so excited?' I asked him, 'Is it being at sea or is it all the places we're going to be visiting?'

'Oh,' he replied, his eyes sparkling, 'it's because we'll be visiting the land where Jesus lived.'

That is how it has been with my air-travelling pilgrims too. Some try to conceal it; most do not; but with few exceptions, perhaps none, they are seized with the same thrill of anticipation at the prospect of actually being in the land where Jesus lived. And this is one instance where the arrival is even better than the hopeful travelling.

We usually arrive after dark and, as we come in from the sea, the lights of Tel Aviv spring up spectacularly out of the night to inform us that touchdown is only minutes away. As for the actual alighting, I often wonder to myself if disembarkation at any other airport in the world can possibly match the nerve-tingling excitement of disembarking in the Holy Land. Simply to know that one has set foot on the very country that cradled Jesus and the Gospel is enough to set the pulse racing and the heart throbbing.

Characters in my Groups

The ever-recurring thrill of leading a group of pilgrims to the Holy Land is partly created by the potential variety of the people who will make up the party. Every group is sure to have its own distinctive character and most groups turn out to have their own particular 'characters' as well. My groups have had their share.

Although there are frequent exceptions, most of those who elect to book on a specifically Christian pilgrimage are committed Christians and churchgoers. It might be expected, therefore, that no pilgrim will ever make life the slightest bit more difficult for the leader than need be. The reality, unfortunately, sometimes presents a different picture. Believe it or not, dear reader, more often than not my pilgrim groups have contained at least one member who proved rather awkward in one way or another, difficult to please, inclined to complain and generally giving the leader a hard time.

I encountered this stern fact of Holy Land leadership before I ever led a group. On our first pilgrimage (a marvellous gift from our Youth Fellowship in High Carntyne) my wife, Marion, and I were part of a group under the leadership of Tim Manson, a Presbyterian minister from Muswell Hill in London, a gem of a man and a first-class leader. Another member of the party was a certain Miss B who totally refused to mix socially with the rest of us - would not even consent to join in for the group photograph which is almost mandatory on such trips - and whom little or nothing seemed to please. (She, of course, had to be the one who, on one of our 'comfort stops', emerged from the ladies' toilets with her skirt caught up in her knickers. She paraded around in that embarrassing state of *déshabillé* for a considerable space of time simply because no one could summon up enough courage to inform her.)

Some time afterwards we discovered that on her return home she had written to the head office of the tour company, Inter-Church Travel, to register a formal complaint against Mr Manson and his leadership. I suppose she might well have been going to do this anyway, but her action was no doubt assured by an unfortunate misunderstanding that took place on our final night.

Being the last night, it was decided to have a kind of 'end of term' party. Bottles of soft drinks, wine and beer were bought in and a happy hour or two were spent in song and story. Everyone joined in except Miss B, who sniffed her disapproval and stumped off to her room for an early night.

When the party was over, the rest of us were shooed off to bed while the three men who had organised the evening stayed behind to clear up. When the tidying up was done, one of them had the 'bright' idea of gathering all the empty bottles together and depositing them outside Tim Manson's bedroom door along with a placard bearing the legend, 'Departed spirits - silence, please'.

It was a joke that Tim's sense of humour would have much appreciated. The unfortunate thing was that the jokers confused the room numbers and - yes, they really did - placed bottles and placard outside the room of Miss B. She utterly refused to believe it was anything other than a deliberate attempt to ridicule her. She was furious and she held the leader responsible. Hence her strong letter of complaint. Fortunately, some of the rest of the group got wind of it and wrote in to set the record straight.

In my own leadership experience I have rarely had anyone quite so difficult to contend with but I have not infrequently had someone in the group who was a bit of a 'thorn in the flesh'. In order to achieve maximum success and satisfaction a group pilgrimage requires willingness on the part of the individual to conform in matters of time and procedures and the like. Someone who persists in going his own way regardless of these things can be a severe headache to the leader, as well as possibly depriving the group of some feature of a planned excursion. There are those, it has been said, who are simply not 'clubbable' types - although in the mind of the group leader they might appear eminently clubbable in another meaning of the word.

Such people, however, have always been very much in the minority. Nearly all are enthusiastically co-operative, anxious to extract the utmost satisfaction and enjoyment from their 'journey of a lifetime'. At times, nevertheless, the wonder, the strangeness, the sheer number of places to be visited can lead to added demands upon the leader.

I well recall one dear old lady of an early group of mine who was, as most are, armed with a camera and determined to take back as full a photographic record as possible for her friends at home. But she was clearly not used to taking photographs and was continually seeking my guidance - often at most inopportune moments - as to which shots she should take and from which vantage point.

Her 'Mr Martin, should I take a photograph from here?' soon became an amusing byword among the rest of the group but it could become a bit exhausting for me. Even more amusing was the lady in another group who snapped and snapped incessantly with her camera and who more often than not would come to me afterwards and ask, 'What was that I just photographed? I'd better take a note of it'.

Nearly all of my pilgrims I recall with much affection. A very few may have been 'pains in the neck' but by far the majority added colour and zest to the tour - and joy to me - by their presence and personality. And a good number are particularly memorable.

There was Miss Taylor, for one. I answered the telephone one evening to hear a female voice asking, 'Would you be prepared to take the risk of having an old woman of 83 on your forthcoming Holy Land tour? I would like to join you and, if you'll have me, I'll do my best not to be a hindrance to the rest'. I assured her that, if she was willing to take whatever risks might be involved, then so was I; and so she booked up. As was my practice, I arranged later a get-together of all those in the party who lived in or around the Glasgow area. This was fixed for a Saturday evening in the home of one of my church members who had already been to the Holy Land with me.

I telephoned Miss Taylor, whom I had not yet met but whose possible frailty had given me much thought, and informed her of the arrangements. I also gave her precise instructions as to how to get to our meeting place, including details of the appropriate buses from Glasgow University, some eight miles distant on the other side of the city, where she was to be attending a meeting in the afternoon of the same day.

Came the appointed evening and the appointed hour, and everyone turned up in good time, including Miss Taylor. 'You found your way all right, then,' I said to her, 'I hope you had no difficulty in getting the right bus.'

'As a matter of fact', she replied, 'I did not come by bus. My meeting finished earlier than I expected and since I had therefore plenty of time, I just walked here'.

I realised then that I need expect no trouble in having Miss Taylor keep up with the rest of the group in the Holy Land. In the event, the only trouble I had with her was in holding her back, as she was forever striding out in front.

She was just one of the many colourful characters who have enriched my Holy Land groups. Jamie Stuart was another. One of my own High Carntyne elders (of which church I was minister for 34 years), Jamie had been a

Travels in the Holy Land

professional actor and at the time of his visit with me to the Holy Land had all but completed (with some encouragement from me) his writing of his book, *A Scots Gospel* which has become a minor bestseller. Jamie gives public readings of excerpts from the book and the very first public or almost public reading from it, still then in manuscript, was given by him to members of our group on the verandah of the Church of Scotland Centre in Tiberias overlooking the Sea of Galilee.

Norman Coombs is another who figures on the long list of real characters who have added much colour to my Holy Land groups. Norman - from Rochester, USA is totally blind but he, accompanied by his wife Jean, had by his own testimony the two weeks that were 'the highlight of his life'. Not only so, he himself was a highlight for the rest of us. With Jean's descriptions whispered into his ear aided, I hope, by my comments, Norman often 'saw' the scenes we visited even more clearly than those of us with full physical sight. And he enjoyed every aspect of the tour with such transparent enthusiasm that he uplifted everyone else. Perhaps for most of us the richest memory of Norman is of his ever-present beatific smile becoming even more so as he swam with exuberant delight in the Sea of Galilee.

Emily was another who smiled her way along our pilgrim route in the face of personal difficulties. Slightly spastic and, shall we say, somewhat past the first bloom of youth, Emily was much less than fully mobile, required a wheelchair at the airports and that sort of thing. But she had such grit and such an appreciation of the locomotion needs of the group that we were rarely kept back on account of her disability. And with it all she maintained a smiling serenity that may well have enhanced her enjoyment of the trip. It certainly enhanced ours.

Her smile refused to disappear even after her mishap on the shore of the Dead Sea. We had been to the top of Masada and had now come to Ein Gedi for a swim (float!) in the Dead Sea. Emily had been looking forward to this particular experience immensely and was all excited as we prepared to enter the water. Whether or not her excitement made her careless. I cannot say, but as she made her way from the changing hut to the sea, she brushed against some tall, sharp grasses and cut her leg. It began to bleed quite profusely but she insisted that, blood or no blood, she was not going to be deprived of the long-anticipated treat of floating in the Dead Sea. So, after some emergency bandaging, in she went, smiling all the while.

We had to have a doctor in to see her, of course, just as soon as we returned to our hotel in Jerusalem. He treated her wound, bandaged it properly and ordered her on no account to let it come into contact with water for at least two days. On hearing this instruction, Emily's smile became even wider and, when the doctor had departed, she chuckled to me, 'I'm so glad I did not see him *before* I got into the Dead Sea'.

Characters in my Groups

Much colour has been added to my groups by members who have come from abroad to join them. People like Marion Stevenson from Victoria, British Columbia, Patricia Mills from Australia, Chris Coull from Australia and lots and lots of Americans.

One very special American family were the Collinses - Jerry (Lt Colonel in the US Army, doing a tour of duty in Germany), his wife, Caroline, and their three teenage children. I must confess to being the kind of tour leader who thrives on encouragement and the Collins family did me proud in that respect. Everything and everywhere in my planned programme was marvellous so far as they were concerned, with some places and some experiences just a bit more marvellous than the others. When, for instance, we arrived at the Scottish Centre in Tiberias after spending our first week of the tour in Jerusalem and had all been dispersed to our various rooms, I found that I was in the same block as the Collins family. Caroline came to me from the verandah outside their room in a state of considerable excitement. The verandah looked out across a Sea of Galilee which was indescribably beautiful in the late afternoon sunshine. Her face all aglow, Caroline said to me, 'I thought nothing could possibly match what we saw in and around Jerusalem but this is even more wonderful. Thank you so much for bringing us to this particular place'.

The Collins children were two boys and a girl. Matthew and Chad were the boys and Missy was the girl. Being the only children in the group they were great favourites with everyone else and got on famously with the leader too. They were, however, indirectly the source of great embarrassment to him one day, although the truth is that it was really all his own fault. It was, in fact, due to a lapse of his concentration while playing football with them.

We had gone to make a visit one afternoon to the Garden Tomb in Jerusalem only to find that we had made a mistake about the hours when it was open to visitors. The opening time after the lunchtime closure was not 2.15 as we had imagined, but 2.30. We had arrived very punctually and therefore had fifteen minutes to put in before we could gain admission. Since Matthew and Chad happened to have a ball with them (I wonder if they have Scottish ancestry) they began kicking it about in the open space fronting the entrance. The secluded space in front of the high wall enclosing the garden lent itself quite beautifully to that kind of activity without causing inconvenience to anyone. The leader, it must be confessed, needed little or no prompting to join in. As the minutes ticked by, the game became faster and more furious until suddenly - disaster. The leader's enthusiasm overcame his discretion and he found himself heading the ball so hard and so high that it sailed clean over the wall to disappear on to the other side.

When, shortly afterwards, the Garden Tomb swung open its doors to

23

admit visitors, it was a somewhat shamefaced tour leader who was heard to echo the frequently made plea of his boyhood, 'Please may we have our ball back'.

As perhaps a salutary illustration of how reluctant we sometimes are to profit from experience, I must own up that later in the tour the leader succeeded in kicking that selfsame ball over another wall in an entirely different location. You will no doubt be relieved to learn that it was safely retrieved on that occasion also.

The American connection once led to a trio from Germany joining my group and enriching it considerably by their membership of it. Carol Muhlbauer was an American married to a German and they were resident in his native land. She had heard me preach and lecture - and also talk about the Holy Land - a dozen years earlier at a conference in Berchtesgaden. Out of the blue one day I received a letter from her enquiring if I was still leading pilgrimage groups to the Holy Land. When she received an affirmative reply, she booked up to come with us on the next trip, along with Herman, her husband, and their next door neighbour, Gisela.

Their participation in the group and in the tour was particularly notable by virtue of the fact that Gisela spoke practically no English. In consequence every description and commentary en route were translated into German for her by either Herman or Carol. This was done *sotto voce* and so unobtrusively that it never caused any of us even the slightest distraction. And it was so well done that Gisela was able to say to me - through them - at the end of our two weeks that this had been the most wonderful holiday of her life and that she intended to come back with me some day, bringing her husband along with her.

As might be expected, there have over the years been a fair number of clerics who have accompanied me on my Holy Land trips. One of these was Ian Collins. Ian, a bachelor, had just celebrated his golden jubilee as minister of Darvel Central Church in Ayrshire, his first and only pastoral charge. One of the many presents a loving and grateful congregation had showered upon him was a trip to the Holy Land which he chose to have with me as tour leader.

It was only after the arrangements were all completed that I discovered that Ian had never flown before and was, understandably, more than a little apprehensive about making his first flight at the age of seventy-five. Although I did my best to reassure him, I was very much aware when we boarded the plane at Glasgow for the shuttle flight to Heathrow that he was still more than a little nervous. As soon as we got off the aircraft after our sixty minutes' flight, I saw Ian heading resolutely towards me, clearly intent on speaking with me. My heart sank. Had the experience been more than he could cope with? Was he unable to face the prospect of the longer flight still to come? Was he going to call off even now? What should I do?

My fears were completely groundless. 'I just wanted to tell you, Jim,' he said, 'that that was absolutely splendid. I never imagined flying would be so enjoyable. If the rest of the tour is going to give me as much pleasure as that, I'm in for a wonderful time.'

By his own later account that is exactly what he had. I will long remember some of his heartfelt comments as we proceeded on our pilgrim way, such as, 'I can scarcely believe that I am sitting here having my breakfast and at the same time looking over the Old City of Jerusalem golden in the morning sun'; 'How marvellous to be walking where Jesus once walked'; 'I never dreamed that one day I might be sailing on the Sea of Galilee and yet here I am doing just that'.

His unbridled enthusiasm reminded me a bit of the similar enthusiasm the Holy Land experience produced in Harriet. Even now, nearly twenty years on, Harriet, whenever she writes to me, always makes some mention of the 'wonderful experience' she had in the Holy Land. And yet Harriet, lovable though she was and ever appreciative of anything done for her, was an immense worry and strain all through our two weeks together.

She was totally unknown to me before the tour started but a few days before departure a letter from her sister was forwarded to me from the Inter-Church office, with whom she had booked the tour direct. I felt a chill sense of foreboding as I read, 'My sister, Harriet, who has booked up on the tour to be led by the Rev James Martin, has become extremely forgetful in recent months and is inclined, left to herself, to wander off. She needs careful supervision and I am writing to ask you to ensure that the leader of the party will keep a close eye on her'. If Harriet is as her sister suggests, I wondered, how on earth was I going to cope? With more than thirty other people to look after, it was impossible for any leader to devote to Harriet the special attention she seemed to require.

In the event Harriet turned out to be even more vague and forgetful than I had feared and her propensity for wandering off was strong and constant.

In fact we simply could not have coped had it not been for the very fortunate circumstance that a nursing sister, Christine Coull, who was a member of my congregation, also happened to be in the group, and she took it on herself to take Harriet under her wing. It was an arduous and exhausting task for her and meant the sacrifice of a good deal of her own enjoyment. But it was a terrific boon to me for which I will always be grateful.

The sort of thing that happened with Harriet was that as we walked along, she would catch sight of a bird or a dog, a child or a horse, that

Travels in the Holy Land

captured her interest; and left to herself she would go in pursuit of that interest, totally oblivious to time or place or the group. Christine was continually having to run after her and retrieve her. Without that retrieving she would undoubtedly have got herself lost on every outing we had.

One day we did lose her. It was our 'free' day in Galilee, that is, a day for which no excursions had been arranged, a day which left everyone at liberty to do their own thing - swim, laze, shop or whatever. Since it was a free day, I did not get worried when Harriet did not appear for breakfast at the scheduled hour. But I did think that in her forgetful way she might have muddled the time and so someone went to her room to remind her and found it empty. We assumed that she had gone for a pre-breakfast stroll and had lost count of time.

As time passed, however, Harriet did not appear, and I became increasingly concerned. Tiberias is not a very large town, certainly not in its sea-front area where we were located, but a walk along the front and through the streets failed to produce any glimpse of her. When she was still absent by lunchtime, we were really alarmed. A proper search was now instituted and the police were consulted, but still no Harriet.

All sorts of horrendous possibilities were by now racing through our minds. I think that many of us had got to the stage of fearing the worst - when Harriet returned, towards the close of day with the light failing speedily.

It was difficult to ascertain just how she had spent the day and where she had been. She was unable to furnish us with a coherent story; but by putting together the bits and pieces she divulged we were able to reconstruct the probable scenario.

She had not slept well - mainly on account of a traumatic experience of the day before - and rising early on an exquisitely sun-kissed morning she decided to go for a stroll. In the course of her stroll she made friends with some children and then struck up an acquaintance with their family. They invited her to their home and that is where she was safely and happily ensconced while we were anxiously scouring the shore and the streets of Tiberias.

The previous day had been our Mediterranean day - visiting Acre, Haifa and Caesarea with a picnic lunch beside the sea at Caesarea. After lunch most of the group walked round the excavated Roman/Crusader township with me but a few opted to sit at the shore and bask in the sun. Harriet was one of these and there were others too, not of our group, sunning themselves at the same spot. A peaceful, pleasant interlude was rudely shattered by the raucous revving of a motor bike engine, the violent snatching of a few handbags and a rapid escape on the pillion seat of the waiting motor bike.

It was a carefully planned and swiftly executed raid and, unfortunately

26

for the victims, a successful one. Particularly unfortunate so far as we were concerned in that Harriet was one of the victims. What was worse, she had been unwisely carrying all her traveller's cheques in her bag, most of her cash and, worst of all, her passport.

The rest of the day's programme had to be abandoned as it was necessary to take Harriet to the police station at Hadera to make a statement. I accompanied her while she was interviewed by the police inspector there, and he was splendidly understanding and patient as she told her tale and answered his questions in her own lovable, exasperating fashion. I will never forget, for instance, his attempt to arrive at a precise statement of the value of the traveller's cheques she had lost.

'Do you remember the total value of the traveller's cheques in your handbag?'

'Yes,' replied Harriet firmly, 'there was exactly £125 worth.'

'You are sure of that?' asked the Inspector, writing it down.

'Yes, because I counted it last night and I haven't cashed any today.'

'Can you tell me how it was made up, what denominations?'

'Oh, yes' answered Harriet, without any hesitation, 'it was all made up of £10 cheques.'

To his credit (or was he by this time utterly baffled) the police inspector wrote down this priceless piece of evidence with as much solemnity as he had recorded all that had gone before.

Despite the loss of her passport, we did manage to get Harriet on the homeward bound flight with the rest of us, but it was not easily accomplished. A succession of telephone calls was not enough and on our penultimate day, a Sunday, I delegated my leadership temporarily to a US Air Force chaplain who was a member of the group, Joe Matthews, and took Harriet to Tel Aviv to meet with the British Consul. He had very kindly agreed to interrupt his day off to come in, open up his office for us and issue a temporary passport which enabled Harriet to fly home as scheduled.

The Harriet saga continued. The first Christmas after our tour I got to bed - as per usual after my High Carntyne Watchnight Service for Christmas Eve, with its 'after-refreshments' - around 2.30 am. At 6.30 am I was dragged reluctantly from slumber by the insistent ringing of the telephone. It was Harriet, bless her, wishing me a Happy Christmas and doing so at that time 'in case I was about to leave for an early service'.

She told me at the same time that she had sent a dozen fresh eggs through the post and hoped they would arrive safely. Her parcel, I am afraid, never did reach me but some two weeks later I received a communication from the local sorting office which stated that a package addressed to me had reached there 'in an offensive condition and had had to be destroyed'. It was clear that the eggs had become scrambled in transit.

Travels in the Holy Land

I have not seen Harriet since our pilgrimage but I still hear from her.

For the majority a trip to the Holy Land is, for one reason for another, a once only experience. Many people, however, do return and some go back over and over again. One of my 'repeat' pilgrims was John Sergeant, whom I have already had occasion to mention. He came to the Holy Land no less than six times with me and was on the eve of his seventh visit when, sitting in his garden one sun-kissed afternoon, he suddenly and quietly slipped away to make the greatest pilgrimage of all.

John nearly never came to the Holy Land at all. He and his wife were contemplating joining my next group when Jenny took mortally ill and soon afterwards died. John was devastated and his friends wondered if he would ever manage to cope with his loss. He had understandably lost all enthusiasm for the Holy Land trip which he had planned to share with his wife; but nevertheless he decided to proceed because he felt this was what 'Jenny would have wanted him to do'.

He came along that first time very fearful that, lacking Jenny, the whole trip would be a harrowing experience, perhaps unbearably so. On the contrary, his fears proved completely groundless and the pilgrimage transformed him. He returned home a new man both physically and spiritually; and he simply could not get enough of the Holy Land after that. It had done so much for him and meant so much to him that he kept on husbanding his financial resources so that he might be able to go back and back.

John Sergeant returned from that first Holy Land pilgrimage so much strengthened inwardly by the experience that he proved a tower of strength to many others in later years. One of those who were helped in this manner was Walter Cumming. Walter had suffered devastation similar to John's with the death of his wife; and his two sons combined to finance him a place on the tour I was leading that same year, in the hope that it might be of benefit to their father. Knowing the circumstances, I managed to arrange that Walter and John should room together. It turned out a very happy arrangement. Walter found in John an understanding as well as a congenial companion, and they struck up immediate friendship which greatly enriched both of their lives.

On his various trips with me to the Holy Land, John was a great help to me too, and in many ways. He was always kind enough to maintain that he owed a large debt of gratitude to me but there was at least one occasion when I must have exasperated him to a considerable extent, although he did not betray this in the slightest.

Normally the group leader has a room to himself, unless his wife is travelling with him. In view of the planning, organisation and administration which are his necessary responsibility, it is extremely important that he should. Occasionally, however, circumstances may decree that he is asked to share a room for one or more nights with another (male) member of the group. One year in Tiberias, when there was a temporary rooming difficulty, I shared with John Sergeant for a few nights.

With characteristic politeness (or deference to the cloth?) John insisted on the first night that I have first use of the shower. It so happened that the electric light bulb in the shower room failed to function; but rather than get dressed again and go looking for a bulb replacement, I decided just to go ahead and shower in the near darkness. We had had a rather long and sticky day (our transfer day from Jerusalem to Galilee) and I thoroughly enjoyed my shower. In the darkness, however, I was totally oblivious to the fact that something was blocking the outlet pipe of the shower cubicle and preventing the water from draining away. What made matters worse was that the retaining border of the shower area had no great depth to it. The result was that very soon - unknown to me - the water began to spill over the retainer and gradually cover the bedroom floor.

When I emerged bright and breezy from my shower I found the floor awash and John desperately attempting to mop up. So far it had been a kind of King Canute effort but now that the shower was turned off and with the assistance of another mopper in the person of myself, progress was made. Most movable objects, including suitcases and footwear, were speedily rescued and placed above water level and gradually, ever so gradually, the water which had reached a depth of an inch, was removed altogether - although, despite our best efforts, much of it found its way under the bedroom door and down the stairs to the consternation of hotel staff and guests.

No one seemed greatly impressed by my timid suggestion that it was the sort of mishap that could have happened to anyone and somehow when we finally sat down to dinner, I found that my appetite had vanished. Poor John Sergeant never did get *his* shower.

John had, as everyone has, his favourite Holy Land places. One was Abu Ghosh, a possible site of the Emmaus story and to many a probable one. It is my habit to gather the group round the open spring which flows beneath the altar in the crypt of the Crusader church there and read the Emmaus narrative, followed by a prayer and singing. John, himself a fine bass singer and a member of our High Carntyne Church choir, always requested that we sing there the twenty-third psalm to the tune of Crimond.

During his various visits John made a number of enduring Holy Land friendships. One was with Hamid Essayad from the Mount of Olives who for many years was my guide in the Jerusalem area. On the tour that immediately followed John's death, Hamid as usual greeted us on our arrival at our Jerusalem hotel. After embracing me he at once looked round for John, knowing that he was to be in the party. When I broke the news to him of John's sudden passing, he was unable to hold back his tears. Later, when in the course of the tour we came to Abu Ghosh, Hamid whispered to me as we were making our way down into the crypt, 'Please sing "The Lord's my shepherd" for John'. With a brief word of explanation to the group, we did just that.

Ever since that day, when year by year my group gathers round the spring in the crypt at Abu Ghosh and the triumphant affirmation is read afresh, 'It is true. The Lord is risen', that same little observance is repeated, whatever the composition of the group. I briefly tell of John Sergeant, pilgrim *par excellence*; we give thanks for him and for all other erstwhile Holy Land pilgrims now walking in the nearer presence of their Lord; and then we sing Crimond once again.

Not Always Smooth Running

Leading a Holy Land pilgrimage is, and must be, a labour of love. Otherwise it is likely to become an almost unbearable chore. If you, dear reader, will now get your handkerchief at the ready and have the violins strike up a plaintive melody, I will proceed to tell you that for the tour leader there is invariably a great deal of hassle and exasperation as well as an enormous amount of hard work and fatigue-inducing responsibility. In addition, on every tour a number of unpredicted and often unpredictable difficulties arise.

It is of some of these unpredicted elements that this chapter is about to speak. But before going any further, let me put the record straight by affirming that so far as any leader worthy of his salt is concerned, that opening paragraph gives only part of the picture, and only a minor part at that. Leadership of a Holy Land pilgrimage can be, and nearly always is, an immensely satisfying and enriching experience. At the same time it does frequently bear out in its own way the truth of the old adage that 'the path of true love never runs smooth'.

Some accidents are virtually bound to occur when a group of thirty or more people go touring for some two weeks in a foreign country. The suprising thing is, perhaps, not that accidents sometimes occur but that so few do. At any rate this has been my experience; but there have been some, mostly of a minor nature, a fall here resulting in some cuts and bruises and a stumble there resulting in a ricked ankle.

There was one in an early tour which was more dramatic and rather more serious. We were visiting the Garden of Gethsemane after dark, for prayers among the olive trees there (such nocturnal visits to Gethsemane are rarely possible nowadays). When the prayers were concluded and we prepared to leave, the group was warned to be careful not to take too sharp a turn to the left as they went out of the gate. A fairly deep trench had been dug there that day in the course of some drainage improvement work and was still open. Despite the warning Jean stepped smartly through the gate, turned even more smartly left and plunged more sharply still into the open trench.

At once a whole battery of electric torches focussed upon the scene to reveal Jean stretched full length on her back in the trench and, as we soon discovered, wedged as tightly as any cork was ever wedged in a bottle. By good fortune we had a medical doctor as one of the group. Although the unfortunate lady's position in the trench clearly made a proper examination impossible, he was able to assure us that she appeared to have suffered no major damage and might, therefore, safely be taken to the hotel where a local doctor could attend to her.

Extricating Jean from her predicament was, however, far from easy. She must have fallen with remarkable precision right into the very middle of the trench. At any rate her body was fitted into its sides so snugly as to make it an extremely difficult task to get her out without causing further injury to her. It looked for a long time as if she would never be released but in the end the operation was completed successfully and Jean was free. But then she found that she was unable to put her left foot to the ground without suffering agonising pain and, sure enough, when we had transported her by taxi back to our hotel and called in a doctor, he diagnosed a severe ankle sprain.

The upshot was that she was confined to the hotel for the next three days before she was able to resume active participation in the tour.

Few tours emerge completely unscathed from some little incidence of minor stomach upset of the kind often referred to in offhand fashion as 'gyppy tummy' or 'the runs' or 'the trots', in a futile attempt to disguise the discomfort and inconvenience of the condition. Unpleasant though this affliction is, it is not a major calamity, not usually anyway. But there was one year when my tour was in the month of July, a much warmer season than my usual time of May or September. Unfortunately our stay in Jerusalem coincided with the outbreak of an epidemic of stomach upset in the city, tracked down eventually to a 'bug' which had got into the city's water supply.

Our group did not escape. Of the total complement of 37, only 5 did not succumb. The leader was fortunate enough to be one of the five and he was even more fortunate to number in the group two nursing sisters. Several of those afflicted were quite ill, two of them very much so, and were confined to bed for a few days. For those few days our section of the hotel was for all the world like a collection of hospital wards. Each morning the doctor made his rounds of room after room with Sister Lynn and Sister Coull at his side.

Not Always Smooth Running

It was a distressing time, and for a period a worrying one, but happily all the patients made a full recovery and some of them even returned a year or two later to the Holy Land for another tour. Happily also none of my other pilgrimages has had anything like the same experience. Minor mishaps, of course, did happen but some of them, it must be said, were self-induced. There was the astonishing occasion when a very sensible and highly intelligent school headmaster appeared to have a sudden mental aberration one hot evening when we were strolling round the Old City of Jerusalem. Feeling the need of refreshment, he insisted on buying some attractive-looking figs from an open stall and eating them on the spot despite my dire warning about the dangers of consuming unwashed fruit. The consequence was that he spent the following two nights and days in a state of considerable distress, although he still maintains it really had no connection with his eating the figs.

On two occasions - *only* two, I should say, for it is probably something to be grateful for, considering the number of tours I have led - punctured tyres played a part in the scenario. Time is usually a matter of prime concern in our Holy Land touring and these two occasions were no exception.

On the first of them we were making a morning, half-day trip from Jerusalem to Jaffa in a brand-new (first time on the road) touring bus. The mishap overtook us when we were less than half an hour's drive short of Jaffa. It was, of course, an unpleasant surprise that our vehicle should sustain a puncture on its maiden tour. It was even more of a surprise, and equally unpleasant, to discover that our driver was unable to change the wheel because he could not lay hands on the tools required to do the job. This shiny, brand-new bus did not seem to carry with it the implements needed for such an undertaking. The driver, at any rate, was unable to find any. As some of us disembarked from the bus and watched his increasingly frantic but vain efforts to locate the tool kit which he kept insisting must be carried by the bus somewhere, we became more and more conscious of the way in which our limited time was steadily slipping past. Just as we had more or less abandoned hope of ever seeing Jaffa that morning, deliverance came in the person of a thirteen-year-old boy. The driver's nephew, he had been given permission to make the trip with us and had been sitting at the rear of the bus. When, after a time, he too came out of the bus to see what was holding us up, he revealed that he was in one respect at least more acquainted with the mysteries of the new bus than his uncle was. He was immediately able to point out where the tool kit was - rather cunningly and invisibly stowed - and soon we were once more on our way.

The other flat tyre incident took place during a taxi ride from Tiberias to Mount Tabor. At that time a visit to Tabor, the traditional mountain of the transfiguration, was not an integral part of our Holy Land tour but an optional extra. We hired taxis to the number required to take us to the top of the mountain, allow us an hour there and then return us to Tiberias. On this particular trip the taxi I was in contracted a puncture when we were only fifteen minutes into our journey. That was unfortunate enough. What complicated the situation further was that ours was the last taxi in the convoy, the normal practice of the leader being to see all others off before embarking himself. The other taxis, consequently, were all speeding on their merry way, quite oblivious to the fact that we were temporarily immobilised. This meant that they would arrive at the top of the mountain some time in advance of us and be able to do little more than hang around rather aimlessly until we arrived, as I was needed to guide them around.

The twenty long minutes it took the driver to change his wheel as we stood at the roadside in the heat of early afternoon seemed like an eternity. The poor, harassed and slightly fuming leader was beginning to dread that the fine enterprise he had so skilfully and meticulously planned was irretrievably ruined when, lo and behold, the wheel was changed, we were back in the taxi and on our way again - on our way to rejoin our by now bewildered and anxious advance party who, of course, had no idea what was delaying us. In the end all was well.

All ended well, too, the time we found ourselves despatched from Jerusalem for six days in Galilee with an Israeli bus driver who knew little English and was acquainted with none of the touring routes, never having driven a tour bus before. Such experiences, I am glad to say, are now far in the past but in my earlier days of Holy Land pilgrimaging the mechanics of the tour were sometimes much less efficiently organised than is the norm today.

On this particular occasion the coach driving arrangements left a lot to be desired. As was the usual practice on our day of transfer from Jerusalem to Tiberias, we put our baggage out before going for breakfast and immediately after breakfast took our seats in the bus in which the baggage had already been stowed. And so we set off precisely as scheduled at eight o'clock. Up till then there had been no opportunity for me to have any conversation with our driver beyond ascertaining - always my first enquiry - that his name was Abraham. It was, therefore, only when we were already on our way that I discovered to my utter horror that Abraham's English was almost as limited as was my modern Hebrew. In consequence verbal communication between us was almost impossible. Nowadays an English-speaking driver is obligatory on such a tour and even then was customary. My heart sank when I realised the difficulties that lay ahead and it hit the floor when I came to recognise that Abraham had previously driven only buses plying locally in and around Jerusalem, and that this was his very first excursion as a tour driver. What is more he had not been supplied - or so it seemed - either with an itinerary or with route directions.

Had this state of affairs come to light before we left the hotel, I would have attempted to have an English speaker substituted for Abraham or at least have had the hotel staff outline to him that we were heading for Tiberias and what stops we were to make on the way. As things were it was too late for either of these strategies so that somehow or other Abraham and I would have to muddle along on our own.

Somehow we did but not without considerable wear and tear on both of us. Although it was one of my earlier tours I was fortunate enough to be able to remember our scheduled morning route fairly well. By dint of hand signals to Abraham and a fair amount of dumb show, we succeeded in getting to Nablus and to Jacob's Well there. With somewhat greater difficulty we managed also to get to Sebaste (or Samaria).

It was only now, however, that the real difficulty emerged. For the life of me I simply could not get through to Abraham that we were to head for Tiberias as our place of residence for the next week.

'Tiberias' I said, but Abraham just shook his head uncomprehendingly.

'T-I-B-E-R-I-A-S', I enunciated slowly and deliberately, but the response was just the same.

Several times I tried, each time more slowly and with greater care than the time before, but still without success.

Then I had the idea - which might and should have occured to me much earlier - of pointing out our destination to Abraham on a map. When this was done and my finger indicated the town, situated as it is right on the Sea of Galilee, his puzzled frown vanished and his face broke into a smile as he said, 'Ah, Tiveriya, Tiveriya'.

Tiberias to me, Tiveriya to him. It was all a matter of words, the use of different words and the different use of words, part of the problem of communication. It reminded me of hearing the Very Rev Andrew Herron use to considerable effect the following illustration of the difference it can make to attach the right words to the right situation: 'There is all the difference in the world between a warm welcome and a hot reception'.

Every Holy Land tour leader knows only too well that the itinerary he has sweated blood to construct and which has been so neatly tailored to prompt departures may well have its smooth running dislocated in greater or less degree by the late arrival of the tour bus at the hotel to pick up the group. As the minutes fly past the leader tends to fume with increasing impatience, constantly readjusting in his mind the tight schedule he has so painstakingly put together. No one else ever seems to share his anxiety or his impatience.

Travels in the Holy Land

You may well find him rushing to the desk in his Arab hotel and telephoning the bus company. The response is always very courteous and intended to be reassuring, 'We are very sorry for the delay, sir, but please do not worry. The bus is on its way and will arrive there any minute now'.

Ten minutes later the leader is likely to be on the telephone again, this time to the tour agent, pleading with him to get something done at once. In a moment or two the agent comes back to him to state that he has contacted the bus company and the bus is on its way and should arrive any minute now. The hotel staff meantime are sympathetic but not distressed, 'Do not worry, sir. The bus will come and what is half an hour, or an hour? It is a beautiful morning. Enjoy it'.

The leader's attempts to convey the importance of having the bus here on time make little impression. Why is he so impatient, they wonder. The bus will come eventually. The leader, for his part, may be reflecting ruefully that the wellknown tale often attached to the Gaelic-speaking highlands of Scotland possibly has its true origin in the Holy Land. When a local was asked by a tourist, 'What is the Gaelic for tomorrow?' he replied, 'We do not have a word for 'tomorrow''. There is nothing so urgent in our language'.

True enough, the bus invariably does come and somehow, despite the delayed start, the programme is gone through without any apparent damage except for some fraying of the leader's nerves.

There are occasions, too, as every overseas traveller is aware, when aircraft are delayed. On my first visit to the Holy Land - when my wife and I were members of the group led by the Rev Tim Manson of Muswell Hill - we had to wait in the airport lounge for more than four hours beyond the scheduled departure time before we were called to board. For a couple who had never flown at all prior to this trip it was not the most soothing of experiences.

When we arrived at Ben Gurion Airport, Tel Aviv, we were to be greeted with the news that our plane's departure would be delayed 'owing to the necessity for some engine repairs to be made'. That news was bad enough. What accentuated our concern was that our aircraft was in full view from the window of the departure lounge and we could quite clearly observe the technicians beavering away on it. As hour succeeded hour and they continued to work on the faulty engine, the nervousness of many of the intending passengers noticeably increased; and it was rather a drained complement of passengers that eventually answered the call to board. The fact that we touched down in London in pouring rain, very late at night and with most people having missed onward travel connections seemed almost inevitable. It says much for the unique joy of a Holy Land tour that not one of the group seemed to feel that these tail-end experiences were sufficient to spoil its memory in the least, not even the poor soul who dropped her duty-free brandy as she went through customs and broke the bottle.

The 'failure to run smoothly' syndrome found one of its most dramatic expressions in my spring pilgrimage of 1990. I had a small sub-group of eight flying from Glasgow with me to join up with another thirty-four, mostly strangers to me, at Heathrow. When we disembarked at Heathrow, our Inter-Church Travel representative met us and after greeting us, said to me, 'Your friend Mary from America has arrived. She flew in from the States this morning early and, although she is considerably handicapped, she is confident she can cope with the various itineraries'.

The truth of the matter was that I was not expecting a friend Mary from America, nor was I at all aware that we were to have a handicapped person in the group. This information caused me some anxiety as well as perplexity, feelings which were intensified when we actually met Mary a few minutes later. She was able to walk only with the aid of a zimmer support and, even then, only very slowly, and that, of course, was on the smooth floor of the terminal building. I realised at once that some walking parts of our itinerary would be impossible for her and my heart quailed as I wondered how I was going to manage over the next two weeks with the problems she would present.

It was only too evident that Mary, particularly as she was unaccompanied, was physically unsuited for the kind of tour that lay ahead, which involves a fair amount of walking, some of it over very uneven terrain. How she had been accepted for the tour mystified me until she informed me later that she had not informed the tour company of her disability. Having previously on two occasions attempted to book up for a Holy Land tour and each time having had her application refused, she had on this occasion simply failed to register her disability on the application form.

So there she was, a problem for the leader before the tour had even begun. There was no doubt that for her own sake as well as for the sake of the group she ought not to be coming with us. But she could scarcely be left behind and told to make her way back home to the USA. Whether her expedition to join us was to be reckoned as brave or as foolhardy, the fact was that she was there, she had been accepted for the tour (even if somewhat under false pretences) and she was positively starry-eyed at the prospect of getting to the Holy Land at long last.

And so Mary was in her place on the aircraft when we took off for Tel Aviv. She was not on board, however, when we took off two weeks later for the flight back to Heathrow.

During our two weeks of pilgrimage Mary had a wonderful time and did not miss out on a great deal of the itinerary. The other members of the group

Travels in the Holy Land

were simply magnificent in their caring for her. A wheelchair was borrowed and in it she was pushed here and pushed there, even though the pushing was always difficult and at times backbreaking. Inevitably, there were times when I had to say, to my sincere regret and to Mary's obvious disappointment, 'I'm sorry, Mary, but I'm afraid we have to leave you in the hotel this morning/afternoon. There is just no way you could manage to be along on this particular excursion'. But these instances were comparatively few.

And so we came to our very last night in Tiberias without any major mishap. We were due to rise at 3.30 am for an early departure to the airport and the homeward flight. My wife and I were about to finish our packing, just about 11 p.m., and I was feeling the usual sense of satisfaction and relief that once more the job had been done, and apparently well done, and that there had been no catastrophes. At that very moment the bubble of complacency burst. Jean, another member of the group, who happened to have her room close to Mary, knocked on our door and called out breathlessly, 'Please come at once. Mary has fallen in her bedroom and can't get up'. ·

Full of foreboding, I followed her to find Mary prone on the floor and quite unable to rise. It seemed very likely that she had sustained some serious injury. 'Oh', she cried, 'This has happened to me so many times', a statement which scarcely was calculated to lessen my concern. Then she went on, 'I hope it will not prevent me going to the Oberammergau Passion Play next month'.

We summoned an ambulance which took her to the local hospital where x-ray revealed four fractures of her leg. The x-rays also showed no less than 17 pins in her legs, the legacies of earlier falls. It was only then we discovered she suffered from the condition known as osteoporosis (brittle bones). She was in no condition to have embarked unescorted on a tour such as ours and it was a minor miracle that she had survived 14 days before this accident occurred.

Sadly there was no travel home for her the next day and we had to leave her in hospital, where she spent 10 days before being allowed to fly home to the USA. She wrote to me afterwards to tell me that, despite all this, she carries with her wonderful memories of a wonderful two weeks.

Jerusalem Within the Walls

When you actually visit the Old City of Jerusalem you find, perhaps to your surprise, that describing it as 'golden' is not just the fantasy of the hymn writer or the licence of the poet. It is literal fact. At every hour of most days, from dawn to dusk, the walls encircling the city glow with a golden light that varies in texture at different hours but never seems to diminish in its loveliness.

Within these walls I have shared with my pilgrimage groups many memorable experiences. At the top of that list must stand, of course, the mandatory experiences, the visits to the places that no Christian tourist could be allowed to miss or would be willing to miss.

The Via Dolorosa, with the Stations of the Cross, is one such. I have taken my groups along that 'way of sorrow', the traditional path which Jesus trod on his walk to Calvary, on different days of the week, at different times of the day and at different seasons of the year.

The most stikingly memorable occasion was when we joined in the mammoth and majestic procession that made its way along the route one Good Friday. When we flew out from Heathrow the previous afternoon we did so in pouring rain. When we arrived in our hotel in Jerusalem that night, it was to be met with the news that there had been a spell of wet weather but that the forecast was for a change.

How accurate the forecast proved. Good Friday began and continued with an unbroken blue sky and sunshine. It was beneath the benevolent gaze of that sunny blue sky that my group went along to join the Good Friday procession. As always, it was to begin at 11 a.m., from the courtyard of the Arab school which marks Station One, almost at the beginning of the Via Dolorosa.

We had thought it wise to be in position well before the procession was due to start off and so we were in the courtyard nearly an hour beforehand.

Travels in the Holy Land

Even then it was a seething mass of pilgrims from all over the world. By the time the procession moved off at its appointed hour, there were more than two thousand people forming its column. They had come from all corners of the earth to be part of the Good Friday procession in the Holy City itself. Some of them belonged to groups who had brought with them a large wooden cross which they would carry all the way to Calvary.

It was a deeply moving experience for each and every one in our particular group (unusually an entirely Scottish party on this occasion) to be part of such an international body gathered together in such a special place for such a special purpose. It took a long, long time for that mass of people to ooze its slow way through the narrow streets of the Via Dolorosa and to come at length to the final Stations of the Cross, situated within the Church of the Holy Sepulchre itself.

Although that is how it is usually referred to, this building's proper title is the Church of the Resurrection; and it has long been believed that it marks the exact location where Jesus was crucified and, later on, close by, raised from the dead. The belief would appear to be well founded for there is considerable evidence to support it.

When the church was built - by the Emperor Constantine in the first half of the fourth century, at the request of his Christian mother, Queen Helena - it was erected on the site which intensive investigation had convinced her was the very place where the crucifixion and resurrection had occurred. The chief collaborator in her researches was the then Bishop of Jerusalem, Macarius by name. His careful exploration of all the available evidence, the known facts and the oral traditions led him to the firm conclusion that the location of Calvary was precisely where Hadrian had put up a Temple of Venus around the year 136 AD. The Jerusalem Christians of the time appear to have been in complete agreement with Bishop Macarius and Queen Helena on this matter.

It may well be, as many have thought, that Hadrian's action in building a pagan temple on a spot held sacred by Christians and regularly venerated by them was a deliberate attempt to defile it, and by obliterating it from sight to obliterate it from memory. If so, it is one of the great ironies of history that what he did had the opposite effect to what was intended and merely marked out the site more clearly for future generations.

Constantine, then, proceeded to build a church there 'to be worthy of the most wonderful place in the world', as he described his purpose in a letter to Macarius. The work was begun under the supervision of Macarius in 326 AD. First of all the Temple of Venus was demolished and the site was cleared. This operation laid bare the rock on which the pagan shrine had been built (believed to be the Rock of Calvary) and also an old tomb which it was thought could have been the Tomb of Christ. The church which

40

Constantine now had built on the site was constructed to enclose both the Rock, cut to form a cube about eighteen feet by fifteen, and the Tomb.

Today you will find the Church of the Holy Sepulchre standing on that very same spot, although it is no longer identical with Constantine's church. The original building suffered much damage and much change as the centuries rolled across Jerusalem. The most substantial of the changes was that brought about by the Crusaders. When they captured Jerusalem, they did not count the Church of the Holy Sepulchre they found standing there to be an edifice worthy of the great events it commemorated.

And so the Crusaders rebuilt it. That was in 1099 AD. What is to be seen there today is in very large measure the church they built, despite the accidents and enforced alterations of the intervening centuries. But, despite its profound significance, it is not an appearance pleasing to the eye, either outside or inside, and is therefore a source of profound disappointment to many first-time Christian pilgrims.

Many are disappointed, too, and more than a little bewildered, to find that the church which is supposed to stand upon the site of Calvary is actually inside the walls of present-day Jerusalem and not outside them as the Gospel narrative has led them to expect. This, however, is something that is easily explained. The fact is that the city walls have changed their line several times in the course of the centuries, and where the Church of the Holy Sepulchre stands today was outside the walls at the time of the crucifixion. We must not forget, after all, that Bishop Macarius and those who agreed with him in the fixing of the site of Calvary were perfectly well aware that the Bible record makes it plain that Jesus was crucified outside the city. It is out of the question to imagine they could have selected a site for Calvary that had been inside the city in the time of Jesus. There can be little real doubt that they chose the correct site.

The fact remains, nevertheless, that the church which occupies the site today is unattractive to look on and is a severe let-down for many expectant visitors. This was brought home to me very forcibly on one of my earlier tours when I came upon a fellow Church of Scotland minister sitting on a bench inside the church with his head in his hands and a look of anguish on his face. (He was part of a pilgrimage group touring the Holy Land under the leadership of my very good friend and outstanding pilgrimage leader, the Rev James Currie.)

'What's wrong, John?' I enquired, 'Are you feeling ill?'

'I'm all right physically', he groaned, 'But I'm absolutely disgusted with this ugly building which marks the place where Jesus was crucified. I just could not take any more and I decided to let James and the others go on without me while I wait for them here.'

I tried to comfort him as best I could. 'I agree it's not the prettiest of buildings', I said 'but in the Holy Land we've always to try to see the holy thing behind the holy place. Often it's not what we are looking at that is the really important thing. It's what it stands for.'

I do not know how much, if anything, my words were of help to him but I have often spoken in similar terms to my groups at that same spot. For it sometimes requires a conscious effort in order to overcome the severe disappointment that first-time pilgrims often encounter there.

Illogical and unreasonable it may be - and undoubtedly is - but many Christians approach the location of the crucifixion of Jesus with a sort of expectation, in spite of themselves, that what they will see will be some kind of 'green hill' akin to their mental picture of the place of his execution. The fact is quite different and to many rather repellent. The building, although steadily being improved in appearance both outside and in, is displeasing and more often than not requires, on first acquaintance, a deliberate endeavour to bear in mind that it reminds us that Jesus gave his life to save the world - and very probably marks the spot where he did.

To remember this is usually to be deeply moved in that place, despite any reservations one may feel about the building itself. Not least when the group sings together in the Chapel of Calvary itself, 'When I survey the wondrous cross', which is something we usually try to do.

As you might guess, our singing in that dimly-lit spot, unaccompanied and highly charged with emotion, would not normally be of the quality to win an award at a music festival. On one occasion, however, no doubt indicating the generous heart of the man, our singing received a commendation from, if I may be permitted to name drop, no less a person than that very popular singer and broadcaster, Sir Harry Secombe.

The Chapel of Calvary is reached from the floor of the church by ascending a flight of very large and steep steps. One of my party did not feel up to tackling the steps and stayed behind while the rest of us visited the Chapel. As she waited below, she was, so she told us, thrilled to hear us singing 'When I survey'. She was even more thrilled as she stood there, that Harry and his wife passed along, escorted by a guide who was conducting them on a private tour. Harry said to her as he passed, 'That's a lovely sound. I wish I had been up there at the same time as the group so that I could have joined in.'

We do not usually sing when we visit the little church the Ethiopians have on the roof of the Holy Sepulchre but our visit there tends to be fraught with emotion, too. Sadly, as most people are aware, the story of the Church of the Holy Sepulchre has been shamefully punctuated over the centuries by squabbles among the various Christian denominations. For many hundreds of years the several parts of the interior of the church were divided between six churches - the Latin (Roman Catholic), the Eastern Orthodox, the Armenian, the Coptic, the Syrian, the Abyssinian.

Each church was very jealous of its rights and sought to guard them vigorously, even to the point of unseemly and bitter public altercations. Somehow in the ongoing process of internecine warfare the Abyssinian or Ethiopian church one day found it had been ousted from the territory it had held in the Holy Sepulchre building. They might have been expected, once it became clear that their dislodgment was irreversible, to steal back to their homeland with as little fuss as possible. Instead they took up residence on the very roof of the Church of the Holy Sepulchre. They remain there to this day. Their small and very humble stone dwellings are situated in the flat courtyard that surrounds the dome of the Chapel of St Helena and their little church is there, too.

The Ethiopians are a gentle community, some two hundred in number, and always have a ready smile and welcome for any pilgrim groups like ours who happen to drop by. It is not necessary to pass through the Ethiopian community when 'doing' the Stations of the Cross, but I, like many another, always choose to do so. This is not merely for the sake of letting the group see these humble, shy people for themselves and the unpretentious, even primitive, dwellings that house them, but also so that we might briefly share worship with them.

Friendly and welcoming as they are, they are always willing for us to crowd into their small chapel set in the corner of their courtyard village. There we engage in a short act of corporate worship of sorts. One of the Ethiopian priests reads a portion of the passion narrative from their own beautifully printed and decorated Bible, and therefore in their own language. I follow by reading the same passage out of my English Bible. At any rate I read what I hope is the same passage, because I speak nothing of their language and they speak very little English. Communication is therefore far from easy and cannot always be trusted as precisely accurate.

No matter, it is an act of solidarity of faith which in the context of their banishment to the roof of the Holy Sepulchre most of us find moving and which, we hope, they may find a source of encouragement. The scripture readings over, I lead a short prayer in which we give thanks for the witness of our Ethiopian fellow Christians and commend them to the love and mercy of Almighty God.

Another very interesting place situated on the Via Dolorosa which we always visit is the Ecce Homo Convent. Belonging to a French order called The Little Sisters of Zion, it stands over the spot where, many believe, once stood the Judgment Hall of Pontius Pilate. That is why the convent has been given the name it bears, for Ecce Homo is Latin for 'behold the man', the words used by Pilate with reference to Jesus as he stood on trial before him (John 19.5).

Underneath the convent one of the things that excavations have revealed is what is called the *gabbatha* or lithostratos, paving stones that were possibly - some think probably - part of the very courtyard of the Governor's residence in Jerusalem. When we descend to that part of the building and stand on these ancient stones, it is with awe that we reflect that we may well be standing just a few yards from the very spot where Jesus was condemned and started his slow march to Calvary.

There are many other interesting features of a visit to the Ecce Homo. Not least is the enormous underground cavern below the convent which, filled with water, presents a very spectacular sight. It not only supplied the water required for Pilate's garrison in Jesus' day, but for some years after its discovery earlier this century it provided for the Ecce Homo inhabitants a source of water that was superior to what the modern city facilities were able to provide.

One of my most striking memories of the Ecce Homo, however, reaches back to one of my earlier visits. Nowadays, following recent extensive work on the archaelogical aspects of the site, particularly with regard to the water cistern, each group leader is left to pilot his group round and give the necessary explanations. In earlier years one of the Sisters, perhaps even the Superior, would do this.

On one of these early occasions of mine when, as it happened, the bulk of my group were Scots, the Sister who escorted us round gave her fascinating expositions in a very pronounced Scottish accent. When we came near to the end of the tour and were standing at the lithostratos, I said to her, before I began the short devotions I like to lead there, 'You are clearly a fellow-Scot. Where are you from?'

'I'm from the Partick district of Glasgow,' she replied in the same soft Scots tongue.

'You can't be long away from Partick,' I ventured to say, 'With a Scots accent so unimpaired as yours.'

She laughed. 'It's twenty years', she said, 'Since I was last in Scotland and I've been in Australia for most of that twenty years.'

Not every encounter I have had within the walls of the Old City of Jerusalem could be said to have the same high spiritual quality as that one undoubtedly had. But most of them have their own special interest.

Charlie was a shopkeeper of the Via Dolorosa whose selling tactics were not hampered by over-zealous concern for strict truth. I allow my groups only very restricted shopping time in the course of a morning or afternoon itinerary. But on this particular afternoon we had completed all our scheduled programme and were using the time still available to amble leisurely along the streets of the Old City.

It was soon after the American air strike against Libya. In the aftermath of this there had been wholesale cancellations of American tourist trips to the Holy Land and the shopkeepers as well as the hoteliers were feeling the financial pinch very much indeed. This had the effect of pushing Charlie out into the street touting for business even more enthusiastically than at normal times.

'Come into my shop. I have very good bargains', he called out at the top of his voice when he saw us approaching. Then he addressed me directly, 'Tour leader, they are tired and need a drink. Bring them into my shop and I will give them tea or cold drinks and they can see the good bargains I have. No need to buy and no charge for looking.'

It had been a fairly full afternoon and the promise of a drink (free at that) was attractive to all. And so, rather against my better judgement, because I had met Charlie before, I gave in and let them all troop into Charlie's shop on his assuring me that the drinks would be along in a very short time.

'While we're waiting for your drinks to come', said Charlie, 'Let me offer you a very special bargain. These silver goblets I am unwrapping are £40 each but trade is so bad due to the many tourist cancellations that I will let you have them for what they cost me - just £20 - just to get them sold. Aren't they really beautiful, Mr Martin?' and he handed me one to examine.

'Charlie', I protested, 'they can't possibly be sterling silver at that price.'

'Oh yes, they are', he pleaded, 'I swear it. I wouldn't tell you lies.'

I was still turning the goblet over in my hands when suddenly I noticed that on the underside it was inscribed EPNS. 'Look here, Charlie,' I called out amid the general hubbub of my chattering group, 'look at this. You see, it is not genuine silver.'

Quick as the proverbial flash, Charlie came back, 'That does not mean the same here as it means in your country. Here these letters mean Excellent Perfect Natural Silver.'

He spoke with great conviction but quite failed to convince and even when he brought down the price of his 'silver' goblets to £6 each, he failed to sell even one. He was more than a little disappointed, not least at my failure to help promote sales, and eventually we all trooped out again from his shop without our refreshing drinks.

At the same time it must be said that the shops and the shopkeepers are a fascinating feature of the Old Jerusalem that is the city within the walls. Every shopkeeper is, of course, out to make a living for himself and his family. That is why he is in business. He is not there simply for the pleasure and the profit of the tourists, although you will meet some who speak as if they are. However, not all shopkeepers, thank God, are as aggressive or insensitive in their salesmanship as Charlie.

The shops in the Old City add so much colour to the tourist's view of it and give it something of its special character. For me, for instance, it is always thrilling to walk through the *souk*, the market thoroughfare. The street here is roofed over - this was done by the Crusaders eight centuries ago - and the shops crowd together jostling each other for breathing space. Usually thronging with people in the daytime, progress along its length can rarely be hurried. This enables us to absorb the atmosphere all the more wholeheartedly, not least the special spicy aroma which is unlikely ever to be forgotten.

While most of the shops are concentrated in the *souk*, the Old City contains shops in other places, too, particularly around Herod's Gate, Jaffa Gate and Damascus Gate. Not the least interesting of these for us Westerners are the shops of the money-changers which are to be found in abundance just inside Damascus Gate. My personal favourite among them is Victoria's. Victoria has inevitably matured from the slip of a girl I first knew many years ago but she has the same charm of manner and the same shrewd business sense that she had then. And she still gives a rate of exchange that no one else is likely to beat.

Sometimes it has been the unpredictable encounters and the unexpected experiences that have been the most memorable part of an incursion into the Old City. Like the afternoon we met a wedding group just off the Via Dolorosa.

We were making our way down the lane that runs from Herod's Gate to intersect with the Via Dolorosa at a point midway between St Stephen's Gate and the Ecce Homo. Suddenly we found ourselves confronted by an excited and happy bunch of people heading in the opposite direction. In the centre was a handsome, smiling youth and those surrounding him, both men and women, were banging drums and generally making as much noise as they could in a patently most joyful manner.

The young Arab in the middle, we discovered, was a bridegroom about to be married and his companions were following the centuries old custom of escorting him to the home of his bride. They would collect her there, we were told, and then carry her back to the bridegroom's house where the wedding meal would be eaten. We were warmly invited to join in the festivities - and the invitation was obviously sincerely meant but we had to decline reluctantly as we did not have the time.

The two to three miles of thick, high walls running round the whole perimeter of the Old City of Jerusalem do not enclose a massive area but they do hold an enormous amount of interest and fascination out of all proportion to its size.

Jerusalem Within the Walls

I usually have my groups for eight days in the Jerusalem area and, if it were not that there are many other places to visit during that time, most of them would gladly spend every one of these days within the walls.

Despite its unprepossessing outward appearance and rather confusing labyrinthine interior, the Church of the Holy Sepulchre could itself occupy the interested visitor for several days. Whether or not he cares for the way it looks, the Christian visitor can scarcely fail to be enthralled and in most cases deeply moved. For this church, which is one of a number of churches built by the Roman Emperor Constantine at the request of his devoutly Christian mother, Queen Helena, surely does stand over the very place where Jesus was crucified to death and raised from the dead. I have already indicated that Helena's intensive researches established this fact beyond much doubt.

Very close to the Church of the Holy Sepulchre stands the imposing Lutheran Church of the Redeemer whose tower thrusts heavenward higher than any other building in the Old City. When time permits, I like to take my group into that church. Some sit and rest and meditate while those who have the desire, the energy and the breath climb with me the 194 steps that take us to the top of the tower and a wonderful, panoramic view of all of the city and beyond. But perhaps my own most pleasing memory of the Church of the Redeemer is of the day I went there and found a group of children from the school next door in the choir loft practising a hymn for a special service the next Sunday. They sang it beautifully to a familiar old mission tune and submerged me in a happy tide of nostalgic emotion.

It is always an emotional experience, too, for the group to visit the Syrian Church of St Mark which is situated in the Armenian Quarter of the city and near to the Jewish Quarter. Many people believe that this church stands on the site of the house where Jesus held the Last Supper with his disciples. Hanging on the wall is a very ancient painting on leather of the Virgin and Child which, according to an old tradition, was painted by St Luke. But the most moving feature of our visit here is to have the priest read the account of the institution of the Lord's Supper from his own scriptures whose language is very close to the Aramaic which was the native language of Jesus; and then to walk in silence and in contemplation through the Jewish Quarter, out of the city and down the hillside in the darkness of the night to Gethsemane, just as Jesus had done on the first Maundy Thursday evening.

The Temple Area is one of the 'musts' for any visitor to Jerusalem. This is a huge esplanade which roughly covers an extent similar to that occupied by the Temple and its environs in the time of Jesus. Its vast spaciousness comes as a striking contrast to the narrowness and the congestion of the Old City streets. And set in the middle of that vast space are the two Moslem sacred edifices of El-Aqsa and the Dome of the Rock, both of them very striking buildings.

47

Travels in the Holy Land

In its present form dating back to the eleventh century, The El-Aqsa mosque is no mere ancient shrine but a place of vibrant daily prayer. It has the space to accommodate several thousand worshippers at once, and frequently does. There are many sights within this vast mosque that are likely to make the visitor catch his breath in awe - the luxurious carpets, for instance, or the superbly beautiful windows of coloured Hebron glass which adorn the building on every side. But none could be more breathtaking than that of some four thousand Muslims kneeling in prayer, covering the whole area in mathematically precise lines.

The Dome of the Rock, on the other hand, is not a place of regular public prayer such as El-Aqsa is. It is essentially a holy shrine, the third holiest in the Moslem world, and a very beautiful building both inside and out. Dating back to the seventh century, it is still very much the same building as was erected then, despite having suffered from earthquakes and other ravages through the centuries since. Its dome, for instance, is now covered with gold-plated aluminium and not with real gold as it was in the beginning; but it cannot surely be any less striking than it ever was, when it shines with golden light in the sun, above the octagonal-shaped, lovely building it surmounts. And inside, the rich carpets, the exquisite windows and the magnificent cupola make it one of the finest spectacles most of us are ever likely to see.

Enclosing the Temple Area on its western side is the Wailing Wall, or to give it its more correct appellation, the Western Wall. This is much revered by the Jews and is for them a special place of pilgrimage. It is believed that the bottom two layers of massive stone blocks may reach back to the Herodian Temple. Devout Jews come here in vast numbers to pray and to lament the destruction of the Temple (hence 'wailing' wall).

From 1948 onwards when the land was partitioned following the cessation of the British mandate and the conflict that ensued, no Jew was able to come to the Wailing Wall since it was part of Jordan. This gave rise to great sorrow and to great longing among multidudes of Jews. This explains why, on 7th June 1967, when the Six Days' War came to its climax in the Holy City itself and the issue was seen to be certain, many Israeli soldiers forsook caution and stampeded to the Wall even while the bullets were still flying.

I could vividly picture the scene for I had been there with a group less than three weeks before. In my mind's eye I could clearly see the labyrinth of narrow streets that led from the Dung Gate to the Wall; and just as clearly the mass of dwellings jammed together there alongside and on top of one another. But I was never to see those streets or those houses again.

The battle for the city was concluded in decisive victory for the Israeli Army late in the afternoon. Almost immediately - at 6 pm precisely - a message was conveyed by loud hailer to the residents of the area lying between the Dung Gate and the Wailing Wall that they must evacuate their houses by 10 pm. At that hour, the announcement continued, the bulldozers would move in and demolition would begin. Right on schedule that is what happened and by daybreak the houses were all gone.

Never since has any building obscured the Wailing Wall nor has there been any impediment to approaching it. The large area which was once occupied by the multitude of houses is now a piazza fronting the Wailing Wall which is itself partitioned into two unequal parts. The larger section is exclusively for men and the smaller one just as exclusively for women. I sometimes suggest to my groups when I take them there that the reason for the larger space being allocated to the men must be that they are surely the more prayerful sex. Always, however, the women in my group insist that it is simply because men are clearly more in need of prayer.

It was at the Wailing Wall, as it happens, that I lost my Bible and found it again. I carry a Bible with me at all times for the short devotions I like to conduct at various points. On this particular occasion I had taken my group through the Dung Gate to the excavations just inside the city walls at that point, then to the Wailing Wall and after that into the Temple Area, with visits to El-Aqsa and the Dome of the Rock. Then I took them to a cafe for a cup of tea. It was then I discovered that my Bible was missing.

It was my wife's Bible, to be perfectly honest, a lovely India paper volume whose slimness made it very suitable for my carrying it around. To have lost it would be calamitous. I had no idea where I might have dropped or left it but I had to do all I could to try and retrieve it. So, leaving the rest to enjoy their tea, I proceeded to retrace as accurately as I could recall every step I had taken during the previous two hours. Back to the Dome of the Rock - no trace of the Bible anywhere around. Back to El-Aqsa - no sign of it there. Back to the Wailing Wall - and *there* was the Bible lying on the chair where, as I now recalled, I had placed it an hour and a half ago in order to leave my hands free to take a photograph for a member of the group. Would it have lain so long untouched, I wondered, had it been Glasgow or London, Edinburgh or Cardiff?

I was all the more pleased to have recovered it intact because I wanted to read from it at our next port of call, The Church of St Anne beside the Pool of Bethesda, close to St Stephen's Gate. This church is built over the reputed home of Mary, mother of Jesus, and her parents Joachim and Anne. There, with the ruins of the Pool of Bethesda only a stone's throw away, we read the story in St John's Gospel, chapter five, of Jesus healing the paralysed man at the pool. After that we sing a psalm or a hymn; and the church building, one of the best preserved Crusader churches in the land (on a par with that at

Travels in the Holy Land

Abu Ghosh), has acoustics which greatly enhance our singing. On one occasion as we were having similar brief devotions in the church, a large company of people filed in and stood quietly at the back until we were finished. As we left, one of them said to a member of my group, 'That was beautiful. Are you a touring choir?'

Considering that we had not even met together until Heathrow on the way out and, even more pertinent, considering that I was one of the singers, that speaks volumes for the acoustics of St Anne's.

When we leave St Anne's Church and make our exit from the city through St Stephen's Gate nearby, I am likely to indicate the point of access to the Ramparts Walk that is close beside that gate. It is possible nowadays to walk on top of the walls almost all the way round the Old City and it is a very rewarding exercise. It does, however, if I may play with words, involve exercise, for it means a continuous ascending and descending of very deep stone steps which require a measure of fitness and stamina.

But, given the time and the energy, the Ramparts Walk is to be recommended. It offers marvellous views of the city and its surroundings - and what contrasts they provide. Looking outward - the majestic sweep of the Mount of Olives across the Kedron Valley, the hustle and bustle of Salah-Eddin Street, the poignant reminiscences of the Mandelbaum Gate of 1948-67, the restored Notre Dame building which for some period after 1967 still bore the marks of conflict, St Andrew's Church flying the Scottish flag bravely on the far side of the Valley of Hinnom from Mount Zion. Looking inward - the dome of the Holy Sepulchre Church, the white tower of the Church of the Redeemer, the splendour of the Temple Mount with El-Aqsa and the Dome of the Rock, the frenzied activity inside Damascus Gate, the clutter of the backyards, the seeming incongruity of the dense forest of television aerials.

One of the most impressive features of the walls of Jerusalem for me is the Pinnacle of the Temple. As a youngster I used to equate this with some kind of church spire but, in fact, it is that part of the Old City's perimeter wall which is the corner of the Temple Area that overhangs the Kedron Valley. Even today the top of the wall is very high above the ground on the valley side. In Jesus' time the drop would have been several times its present depth - before the steady building up of the valley floor through twenty centuries of human life and history. It was to this 'highest point of the temple' that the Devil took Jesus to tempt him to seek results in his ministry by using his powers to perform spectacular stunts like leaping down into the valley far below without sustaining any damage to his person.

'No, no,' was Jesus' reply, 'My missionary purpose is to win human souls, not to dazzle human minds.'

The Mount of Olives

There are eight gates set into the walls of the Old City of Jerusalem - Damascus Gate, Herod's Gate, St Stephen's Gate (alternatively known as Lions' Gate because of the two pairs of lions carved in the wall above the entrance), Dung Gate (so-called because the refuse from the city used to be carried through it before being flung into the valley below), Zion Gate, Jaffa Gate, New Gate and Golden Gate. The Golden Gate is permanently closed. It has been closed since the departure of the Crusaders and a tradition says that it will remain closed until Jesus returns in Judgment.

Facing the Golden Gate and on the other side of the Kedron Valley is the Mount of Olives, one of the most famous locations in the world and, for Christians, highly charged with emotion. On the very top of the Mount is the Church of the Ascension which marks the traditional site of that event. Below that lies the Church of the Paternoster which commemorates Jesus' teaching of the Lord's Prayer and in token of that has the prayer inscribed on tiles on the walls of the cloisters in around seventy different languages. Lower still is the beautiful little church of Dominus Flevit which marks the weeping of Jesus over Jerusalem.

At the very bottom of the hill, adjacent to the Jerusalem to Jericho road, lies the Garden of Gethsemane. In the time of Jesus the name Gethsemane was applied to a large section of the lower slopes of the Mount of Olives. When the Franciscans, the custodians of many of the Christian sites in the Holy Land, set apart this much smaller area beside the main road as *the* Garden of Gethsemane, they were probably not only wise but also historically correct. It seems highly probable that, when Jesus came out of the city on the first Maundy Thursday evening, down into the valley and across the Kedron brook, he would proceed only a short distance up the slope of the Mount of Olives before he began to agonise among the olive trees prior to his betrayal by Judas Iscariot.

Travels in the Holy Land

On my first visit to Gethsemane in 1965 there were only eight olive trees in the garden, all of them very old. H.V. Morton in his book, *In the Steps of the Master,* maintains that some of them were probably there in the time of Jesus. This is most unlikely. A healthy olive tree, however, may live for eight hundred years and does not die until it has given birth to a successor, a fresh and vigorous new shoot that will in time replace it.

This means that the eight old trees in the garden may well be the grandchildren of the trees that Jesus knew there, only two generations removed from the very trees that looked down upon Jesus in his agony.

Today there are twenty-four olive trees in the Garden of Gethsemane. The Franciscans have added sixteen young trees to the eight ancient ones; but these ancient ones stand out impressively in their venerable antiquity. This is particularly so with what is probably the oldest of them all. It stands closest to the nearby Church of the Agony and from its very heart already there is growing - stronger and thicker each year - the new tree that in time will stand there in its parent's place.

The Church of the Agony is so called because it commemorates the agonising of Jesus in Gethsemane and indeed incorporates before its altar what is believed to be that part of the native rock on which Jesus knelt in prayer before the traitor Iscariot betrayed him with a kiss. The Church is more popularly known as the Church of All Nations because it was built (1921-3) with money that was contributed by many countries. The vast ceiling of the Church high overhead is broken up into a series of smaller cupolae all of which are adorned with mosaics that identify the various nations who were benefactors.

The Garden and the Church are our ultimate goal, our eventual destination, when I take my groups on what we usually call the 'Palm Sunday Walk'. Some of the sacred sites in the Holy Land are purely speculative, some are no more than symbolic or representative; but some can claim a fair degree of historical probability and among these are a number concerning which we may have every confidence. The Palm Sunday Walk belongs to this latter category.

This walk consists of the ascent of the hill behind Bethany, the reverse side of the Mount of Olives, and the descent of the Mount on the other side. As we follow the winding track upwards from Bethany we are without doubt walking where Jesus walked all those centuries ago - at least until we come to Bethphage at which point the rough pathway becomes a modern road.

For me personally this part of the pilgrimage has never failed to be one of the highlights even after many repetitions. The places seen and visited on the way - the Church of St Lazarus, the Tomb of Lazarus, the Church at Bethphage, the Chapel of the Ascension, the Paternoster, the Dominus Flevit, the Russian Church of Gethsemane, the Garden of Gethsemane, the Church of All Nations - all have their own interest and inspiration. But dominating and enriching the whole thing is the awareness of having walked in the very footsteps of Jesus.

It is a wellknown fact that when human feet first climb a hill, or cross a field, or make their way through a forest, they choose the route that is easiest or most convenient; and those who come after tend to follow the way that these pioneer feet have marked out. In a very short time a pathway has been beaten out and this becomes the accepted path for everyone to tread. It would be no different with the climbing of the hill behind Bethany to the crest of the Mount of Olives. We may be quite sure when we ascend that hill today that we are treading the very path that Jesus trod in his time.

At the same time the Palm Sunday Walk can have its lighter moments, too. Directly opposite Lazarus's Tomb is Abraham's shop and when I knew him first, Abraham had a coke-drinking camel. If you cared to purchase a bottle of coke for the camel, opened it and set it upright on the ground in front of him, he would put his mouth firmly over the neck of the bottle, fling his head smartly back and in an instant return the bottle to its upright position on the ground - but empty. When I led my first group to the Holy Land in 1967, it was nearly forty strong and during our short stop there, the camel speedily disposed of exactly that number of bottles of coke. Most enjoyable for the camel, great fun for the tourists, good business for Abraham - but I never saw that camel again. He was one of the incidental casualties of the Six Days' War, just three weeks afterwards.

It was at that very location that I myself became a casualty - a minor one - on a later visit. I had gone with my group down the steep steps into the dimly lit Tomb of Lazarus and decided to hurry back up the steps ahead of them in order to arrange for a demonstration of a 'Davidsling' in action. As I catapulted from the last step into the sunlight, I completely failed to take account of the lowness of the lintel of the entrance to the Tomb and dealt the top of my head a painful crack against the masonry.

There was quite a bit of blood, much consternation on the part of everyone else and a quite enormous amount of embarrassment on mine. After some very kind but very rough and ready (and, I suspected, not altogether hygienic) attempts at first-aid, the walk continued with the brave but foolish leader a bit groggy and with a bandage of sorts adorning his wounded head.

On our return to the hotel, the manager insisted that I see the doctor, which I did. He stitched the wound and covered it with a white dressing that sat on the top of my head like a square of icing on a cake. This had to remain in place for the next three days, which meant that I was thus embellished when I conducted an open-air Communion service the following morning.

When the three days were up the doctor gave his 'all-clear' and the

53

dressing was removed. It was only then that one dear lady member of the group, an Anglican, learned what this protuberance on my head had been. Somehow she had been unaware of my enforced visit to the doctor. 'Oh', she said to me, 'I didn't know what that white thing was. I thought it was some kind of badge of office worn by Presbyterian clergymen.'

It was in the course of this same Palm Sunday Walk - although in different years - that I met with two vivid illustrations of the avid desire for learning that many young Arabs have. On the first occasion, we had just gone a little way above Abraham's shop when a young lad sought to attach himself to me.

'I would like to be your guide up the hillside', he said politely.

'Thank you', I replied, 'But I do not need you to guide us. I am able to do that myself perfectly well. In any case we have no money to pay you for guiding us.'

'But I do not want money', he said. 'I want only the opportunity to practise my English.'

So we allowed him to walk with us for a space and 'practise his English'.

The other occasion was when I fell into conversation at Bethphage with twelve-year-old Hanan. She spoke such beautiful English that I felt compelled to congratulate her.

'You speak English quite beautifully', I said. 'Do you speak any other languages besides your own?'

'Yes', she replied modestly. 'I speak some German, too.'

'Are you as good at German', I asked, 'as you are at English?'

With equal modestly she replied, 'My German is better than my English. In the examinations, I got 92% for English but I got 95% for German'.

My admiration was unbounded for her linguistic prowess, just as it is for the eagerness to master other languages which so many in the Holy Land display. It puts to shame the multitudes like myself who are content to make do with our native tongue in the hope and the expectation that wherever we may go someone there will speak and understand it.

Let me return to the Palm Sunday Walk. When we are 'doing' this walk we start in the heart of the village of Bethany at the modern Church of St Lazarus (built in 1954) situated beside the main road. The church, like so many Holy Land churches, is built on the ruins and over the foundations of earlier churches going back at least to the fourth century. Apart from its own attractiveness, enhanced by its murals reminding us of how Lazarus was raised from the dead by he who is 'the Resurrection and the Life', the church offers us additional interest on account of the remains of its predecessors that are visible to the eye just beside it.

One of my own fondest memories of visiting the Church of St Lazarus at

Bethany is not directly connected with any feature of the Church itself or the relics adjacent to it. It is of Father Agostino who was priest there in my earlier Holy Land years. He had a magnificent tenor voice and had, in fact, served an apprenticeship as an opera singer at La Scala, Milan before turning his back on that to follow his vocation.

He was an adorable man with a twinklingly joyous smile. Although his English was far from fluent and my Italian was non-existent, we somehow established a happy relationship. I discovered that, for the visit of Pope Paul in 1964, he had himself set to music the scripture texts in Latin which accompany the murals in the Church; and he had sung this to the Pope when he had come. I managed to prevail on him to sing it for my group on my second visit as a group leader and on every subsequent visit until he was transferred to Mt Tabor.

The ascent of the hill, from the Church of St Lazarus up past the Tomb of Lazarus and Abraham's little shop, never becomes any less moving so far as I am concerned no matter how often I make it. To be putting my feet on the selfsame rough track as Jesus, long ago, used many a time to put his, is a thrill beyond adequate description.

In a strange way, too, it somehow brings his humanity closer and makes it more real. Periodically I have the group come to a stop for a few minutes. This permits the stragglers - there are inevitably some - to catch up with the vanguard and allows all the party to have a breather. It also permits us to look backwards to the panorama of Bethany lying beneath us and to the wilderness beyond. At the same time it tends to provoke the thought that Jesus in his time may well have stopped here or hereabouts in order to look back at the vista or to draw breath or to wipe his brow on a hot day.

Certainly he would feel, as we were feeling, the sun upon his back and the gentle breeze upon his face. The Palm Sunday Walk often seems to be saying, to me at least, that our Lord Jesus was no mere imitation of a man. Uniquely divine though he was, his humanity was no charade. It was real and so were his sufferings and his death.

But before we get on to this rough dust-strewn track that winds up the hillside above Bethany, we stop for a time at the Tomb of Lazarus. The original entrance to the traditional burial place of Lazarus long ago had a mosque erected over it (because Moslems also venerated the raising of Lazarus) and it is no longer accessible to Christian pilgrims. The Franciscans, however, cut a new entrance to the tomb in the sixteenth century and this makes it possible for us, too, coming so long afterwards, to see it. This is accomplished by descending a dimly lit and steep flight of steps. Once at the foot of the steps we see not only the old tomb itself but also remnants of the crypt of the Byzantine church which once stood there over the tomb.

Travels in the Holy Land

When we re-emerge into the outer air, the leader advises the group to avail themselves of the opportunity to purchase a soft drink in Abraham's shop to guard against any danger of dehydration in the fairly stiff upwards climb that awaits us. While this advice is being followed, Abraham's assistant, happily called David, gives a demonstration of what he calls a 'David sling'.

Most of us, perhaps, when we read of David slaying Goliath with sling and stone, visualise him using the kind of v-shaped catapult some of us knew as boys. This modern day David soon puts any such notions to rights. 'This is the kind of sling that David used', he says, as he holds one aloft. It consists of a woven pouch with strings two feet long attached to either end, each string ending in a loop. Picking up a round stone from the roadway, David places it in the pouch. Then he slides the thumb of his right hand into one loop and his forefinger into the other. This done, he proceeds to whirl the sling round his head faster and faster until, suddenly, he releases one end. The stone swishes away into the air with astonishing speed and reaches a great height before plummeting back to earth.

In the face of our gasps of admiration, David modestly protests that he in fact is not very expert in the use of the sling. But those who are experts, he claims, can project a stone so accurately that they are able to strike and kill a bird in flight. We find it a lot easier after this to picture how David killed Goliath.

And so we proceed on our way.

After about a mile of the rough dust-strewn track, up the hillside from Bethany we come to Bethphage and a modern, tarmacadammed road. Once we have visited the little church at Bethpage which commemorates Jesus' mounting the donkey for his ride into Jerusalem on the first Palm Sunday, I usually lead my group into a house close by. This is the residence of my friend, the guide, Hamid Essayad; and his wife will have ready for us some very acceptable fruit juice.

Hamid's is a very lovely home, three stories high, and is a fine example of the way that Arab families can work together. Over the course of a few years I saw this house arise from a cleared site to what it is now - and it was all a kind of 'do it yourself' project. Hamid, in other words, built the house himself - with the assistance of his brothers and his uncles and his cousins and his nephews and a whole lot more.

First of all he built a ground floor dwelling for himself, his wife and his two sons. Next, having decided it was time that Bassam, his elder son, was married and since it is still very much the Arab custom to have families living under the same roof even after the offspring get married, Hamid built a second storey to his already handsome house. He and his wife moved

56

upstairs leaving the original house for Bassam and his wife. They were duly married and installed in the house and soon began to rear their own family there.

Shortly, Hamid felt it was time that his younger son, Mahmoud (or Mike) should also take to himself a wife; and so another storey was added, with the intention of Hamid and his wife moving yet again upwards. However, to Hamid's intense and continuing chagrin, Mahmoud rebelled and refused to proceed with the marriage which, in line with regular custom, had been arranged for him. And so, at the time of writing, the topmost storey of Hamid's magnificent house is still not lived in.

Nevertheless, the fruit juice continues to be on offer and is always gratefully received. It certainly helps considerably as we complete our ascent of the hill. The road may be much smoother from here on but it is also much steeper and the refreshment enjoyed at Hamid's adds a needed spring to our steps.

What we call the Chapel of the Ascension, on the very summit of the hill, is in actual fact a Moslem mosque. A Christian church commemorating the Ascension was built on the site in the fourth century. This earlier construction was built in a circular shape but nothing remains of it today. The Crusaders replaced it with an eight-sided church whose centre, like that of its predecessor, was open to the sky. After Saladin had defeated the Crusaders and expelled them from Jerusalem, he gifted the site to two of his followers. When the Moslems restored it in 1200 A.D. they roofed it over but retained the rest of it much as it was, and that is how it is still.

This octagon-shaped church-become-mosque which marks the supposed site of the Ascension and commemorates the event, contains what is perhaps the most grotesque relic that we see on our pilgrimage. It is a depression in the rock floor of the mosque (the very crest of the mountain) which an ancient tradition asserts to be the mark of Jesus' right foot. At one time the floor bore the alleged mark of the left foot also but this was cut out during the Middle Ages and transferred to the El-Aqsa mosque in the Temple Area.

From this point on, our Palm Sunday Walk is all down hill, a fact which is always much appreciated by every member of my group. It is also much appreciated by their leader because by this stage of the walk, time is often a very important factor. I invariably 'do' the Palm Sunday Walk with my groups in the forenoon and, although we start off before eight o'clock, we are sometimes a bit pressed for time when we begin our descent of the Mount of Olives.

The difficulty is that most of the places in our itinerary are closed to visitors for a period at lunch time. Dominus Flevit, for instance, closes at 11.30 and the Garden of Gethsemane at 12 noon. It is imperative that we reach these places in good time, otherwise we might fail to gain admission. There is absolutely no possibility of getting into either of these places after these prescribed times, sometimes quite the reverse. I remember once leading my group down the road towards Dominus Flevit. It was 11.10 as I came within sight of the entrance and I thought to myself 'Just in time' as I noticed the priest in charge standing there looking towards us. I was wrong. The priest clearly calculated that to admit us at that time might well incur the risk of not getting us out quickly enough to allow him his full lunch break. At any rate I reached the entrance just in time to hear him lock the gate behind him as he closed up for the morning.

Fortunately I was able to take them back another day because it would have been a pity if they had missed it. Dominus Flevit is such a beautiful church and built on such a magnificent spot.

But I am rushing you on in advance of the group. Before descending to Dominus Flevit we enter the grounds of the Paternoster Church. As the name indicates (Pater Noster is Latin for 'Our Father') this church is there in commemoration of Jesus' teaching of his model prayer to his disciples. Built last century it strikingly symbolises this commemoration by having in its cloister large rectangular frames of tiles that display the Lord's Prayer in different languages. There were around seventy the last time I counted but each year I see the number steadily increase.

The brief devotions we have at the major stops are even briefer here. We gather in the crypt with its relics of earlier churches that once occupied the site, and join in repeating the Lord's Prayer, each in his or her own tradition.

From here we continue down the fairly steeply sloping road. We pass by the Jewish cemetery with its mass of new-looking graves. There are many hundreds of them here on the face of the Mount of Olives and they have all been made since the Six Days' War of 1967 and the subsequent occupation by the Israelis of this part of the land. This does not mean that there has been an astonishingly high death rate in that period. To a large extent they represent the fervent desire of many devout Jews to have their relatives buried within sight of the Holy City; and who have accordingly had their remains exhumed and reinterred here.

A short distance further down the slope brings us to the entrance to the Dominus Flevit. Its name means 'The Lord wept' and it reminds us of Jesus weeping over Jerusalem because it was spurning him and his message. Built in 1955 by the Italian architect Barluzzi, the beauty of its appearance and of its commanding situation is poignantly enhanced when we move inside and observe how its dome of gold mosaic has been constructed to represent a falling tear. This is in keeping with the mosaic on the front of the marble altar which depicts a hen with her wings outstretched to enclose her brood of chickens and has on the circumference of the mosaic the words from the Gospel, 'How often would I have gathered your children together as a hen gathers her brood under her wings and you would not'.

As we depart from the Dominus Flevit and continue our descent we pass beneath the compound of the Russian Orthodox Church of St Mary Magdalene before coming, at the very foot of the slope and right beside the busy Jericho road, to the Garden of Gethsemane with the Church of All Nations adjacent to it.

I remarked earlier on that it would have been a pity for a certain group of mine to have missed the Dominus Flevit. It would be an even greater pity if we ever missed out on the Garden of Gethsemane which always proves to be such a special place for every Christian pilgrim. Whether or not we believe that some of the olive trees in the Garden today were actually there in the time of Jesus, it is not difficult to let imagination take hold in that spot and be transported back across the centuries to the first Maundy Thursday. Even with the constant traffic roaring past on the Jerusalem-Jericho road outside the garden, it is not difficult to visualise Jesus on his knees among the olive trees in the intense agony of bracing himself for the ordeal of crucifixion soon to befall him. As we stand there in the Garden of Gethsemane we can almost see the torches gleaming in the night and hear the murmur of voices borne on the breeze as Judas the traitor leads the high-priest's minions to arrest his leader.

In earlier years we used to be allowed to enter the Garden itself, wander along its paths and have our devotions beside one of its old olive trees. I remember with humble gratitude how I shared in a Communion service once around the oldest tree of them all. We used also to pay a visit there at night. To stand among the olive trees of Gethsemane in the darkness and to project one's thoughts back through the centuries to Jesus agonising in similar darkness there before his betrayal and arrest is a profound experience. Groups are no longer permitted to enter the Garden proper. Apparently - hard and sad to believe - it is because visitors would persist in picking up stones from the paths and plucking twigs from the trees to take home as souvenirs.

Nowadays we can do no more than walk round the ambulatory that encircles the garden but that itself is a thrilling and moving experience, with the colour and fragrance of the flowers enveloping us on all sides and the old olive trees before us seeming to reach back almost to Jesus himself.

It is at first like entering a different world when we leave the bright sunshine of the Garden and go into the church, for the lighting is kept deliberately low in keeping with the dimness of the natural light diffused by the coloured alabaster windows. But it all seems most appropriate for the ending of our Palm Sunday Walk as in that subdued setting we have a prayer and a bible reading and then join in singing:

When I survey the wondrous Cross
On which the Prince of Glory died
My richest gain I count but loss
And pour contempt on all my pride
Love so amazing, so divine
Demands my soul, my life, my all.

Scotland and England in Jerusalem

The Scots and the English have their own churches in the Holy City - or, to be more precise, the Presbyterians and the Anglicans of these two races have.

St Andrew's Church of Scotland stands on an eminence directly across the Valley of Hinnom from Mount Zion, commanding a splendid view of Mount Zion itself, of the Jaffa Gate and indeed of the whole of the Old City on its south-west aspect. It is a memorial church, built 1927-30 in memory of the Scottish soldiers who lost their lives in Allenby's victorious campaign for the liberation of Palestine from the Turks in 1917. The foundation stone was laid by Allenby himself, now Lord Allenby of Megiddo, himself a Scot. That was on 7th May 1927 and the completed church was dedicated on St Andrew's Day, 30th November 1930.

It is hauntingly sad to reflect how this church and its adjoining hospice, erected to honour the dead of one world war, should little more than a decade later be affording comfort and rest to men and women engaged in fighting another. My own brother, George, was one who found a brief but welcome respite here, along with others from his battalion, the Second Cameronians, between the push to Rome that followed the horror of the Anzio beachhead and his death in action in Germany beside the River Elbe in the closing days of the war in Europe. The memory that he visited that Jerusalem Church of St Andrew long after his mother and brothers had seen him for the last time adds special poignancy to my every visit there.

But this is not the only thing that gives poignancy to St Andrew's so far as I and many another Scot are concerned. There is the Iona marble fronting the pulpit, the Iona marble fronting the Communion table and the Iona marble set in the floor behind the table. Of the latter H.V. Morton, in his book *In the Steps of the Master*, maintains it is placed there because the Scots are a sentimental race and this ensures that every time the minister celebrates the sacrament he is aware that his feet are placed on part of his native land. There, too, are the names of the Scottish parishes and other bodies inscribed on the backs of the pew chairs they gifted to the church. And there is the brass plaque in the chancel floor which recalls a piece of romantic Scottish history. It is inscribed: 'In remembrance of the pious wish of King Robert Bruce that his heart should be buried in Jerusalem. Given by the citizens of Dunfermline and Melrose in celebration of the sixth centenary of his death in 1329 - 7th June 1929'. Before his death King Robert requested Sir James Douglas to carry his heart to Jerusalem, in recompense for his unfulfilled vow that he would visit the Holy City. Consequently Douglas set out with the embalmed heart of his king but on the way to the Holy Land he fell in battle against the Moors in Spain. The heart was recovered and later interred at Melrose while the body rests at Dunfermline.

Even more poignant for me is the memory of the time, the only time, I baptised a member of my group in St Andrew's Church. Nearing the end of the first week of our pilgrimage which had been spent in Jerusalem, Helen Thomson told me that the whole experience had made such a difference to her spiritually that she would like very much if I could and would baptise her in St Andrew's. This I readily agreed to do. The minister's permission was also readily granted and it was arranged that I would perform the ceremony at a certain time on our free afternoon. At the agreed hour, we gathered in the church, Helen and myself, along with her sister and her sister's husband and two other personal friends. It was one of the most moving baptismal services I have ever conducted and, shortly, events were to invest it with greater poignancy still. This was in the spring of the year, when Helen was 42 years of age and apparently in the best of robust health. But in September she was diagnosed as having cancer.

She died the following January, much less than a year after our Holy Land pilgrimage. Whenever I visited her, she never failed to speak of that pilgrimage with joy and thanksgiving. On one occasion, near the end, she said to me, 'How glad I am that I went to the Holy Land in your group and how glad I am that you baptised me there. It meant a lot to me at the time. It means even more now'.

Over the years I have participated in many Sunday services in St Andrew's, sometimes simply as a worshipper, but at other times conducting the whole service or preaching the sermon or reading a lesson. All of these have been uplifting to me and some inevitably were more memorable than others.

There was one - it was in 1975 - which so far as I was concerned was probably the most exciting of them all. We had been in Jerusalem for the best part of a week, during which we had visited St Andrew's and also made contact with the minister who was therefore aware that the majority of the group intended to worship there on the Sunday morning. He had asked me to read one of the lessons. On the Saturday evening I was called to the telephone in our hotel. It was the wife of the minister of St Andrew's.

'Tom has gone down with chicken-pox', she informed me, 'Would you help us out by taking the whole service tomorrow morning?'

I had no hesitation in assuring her I would do so. The dire situation demanded it. But I had not thought to pack any of my sermons - why should I? - and so I was considerably later even than usual in getting to bed that night.

From that time on I took the precaution of including a couple of sermons in my luggage - just in case. At times they were needed. Sometimes I knew before I left home that I was to preach (either in Jerusalem or in Tiberias), sometimes I would receive an on the spot invitation.

There were two occasions when a sermon I thought was to be used was brought back home without having been delivered. Tom Houston's successor as minister at St Andrew's was Dr Robert Craig, who had come to it after a most distinguished career abroad and was later to become Moderator of the General Assembly of the Church of Scotland. He was, and is, a most delightful Christian gentleman but, as I discovered, given on occasion to a little absentmindedness.

On my first visit to St Andrew's after he began his ministry there, Dr Craig invited me to read one of the scripture lessons. After the service he said, 'It would be good to have you preach the sermon next time you come. Do you know when that will be?' When I told him my next year's dates were already arranged, he took a careful note of the Sunday I would be in Jerusalem and said, 'That's it arranged. We will look forward to hearing you then'.

When the following year came round and I was once more with a pilgrimage group in Jerusalem, I was at pains to warn all those intending to worship in St Andrew's that they would have to put up with me preaching the sermon. On the Sunday morning when we turned up in good time for the service, I duly had my sermon with me.

As always, Robert Craig greeted us with sincere warmth and to me he said, 'I'm particularly pleased to welcome you back again. Will you be so kind as to read one of the lessons?' And so my sermon notes were never taken out of my pocket. He had clearly forgotten all about the arrangement that had been made.

I made no reference to that arrangement - what was the point? - he clearly had his service all prepared. But when it was over, he said to me 'It's a pity I did not know when you were coming. I would have asked you to preach the

Travels in the Holy Land

sermon. Could we make a definite arrangement now for you to preach on your next visit?'

And so we did just that. I gave him the date of my next Sunday in Jerusalem and he carefully noted it down. I did not have the heart to say that we had been through all this before. In any case, he would not forget again, would he?

In due course, then, I presented myself once more at St Andrew's complete with sermon as well as my group. We were welcomed most cordially by Rizek Aboushar, the session clerk, who said to me, 'Dr Craig is expecting you, Jim. Will you go along to the vestry and see him?' A wave of relief swept over me. This time I had not been forgotten. This time my sermon would not have to be taken back home unused.

'It's marvellous to have you with us again', said Dr Craig as he shook my hand, 'Would you be so kind as to read the New Testament lesson for us? Bishop Muzorawe is here, too, and he has agreed to read the Old Testament lesson' (the bishop had been a close friend of Robert Craig's since Dr Craig's time as University Principal in Rhodesia). Accepting my fate, I made my way to the front of the church to join Bishop Muzorawe - and discovered that he also had been asked to read the New Testament. However, we managed to sort that out very amicably but I never did preach during Dr Craig's ministry in St Andrew's.

Of the many services I have attended, conducted or otherwise shared in St Andrew's Church, Jerusalem, none has thrilled me more either at the time or in retrospect than the one I took part in one Easter Day at dawn. Eastertide is a glorious time for a Christian to be in the Holy Land, although usually much busier and also much more expensive than at other times. I normally take my groups at times other than Easter but I did go once then. How glad I am to have had that experience - and the Easter Dawn service was an exhilirating part of it.

That Easter morning we rose just after three o'clock but this was far from being a matter of dragging ourselves unwillingly from slumber. The fact was that few of the group had slept at all. All through the night of Easter Eve the bells of innumerable Jerusalem churches had been tolling and making sleep virtually impossible for us. Nevertheless it was with considerable eagerness and anticipation, as well as with some feeling of privileged awe, that we got up and dressed. Sunrise was going to be around 4 am and we were aiming to be at St Andrew's shortly after half past three.

We knew that St Andrew's looked straight across the valley to the place where Jesus' crucifixion and resurrection had taken place. We were very much aware, therefore, as we took our seats on the chairs set outside the church on the terrace overlooking the valley that we were directly facing the site of Calvary, even though at the moment we could see nothing at all because of the pitch darkness that surrounded us.

It was, I suppose, a rather prestigious kind of service. Among those taking part were an eminent divine from one of the African churches and our own Andrew Herron in his year of office as Moderator of the General Assembly of the Church of Scotland. It had attracted a fair amount of media attention, too. There was a television unit there from CBC and I remember my young school teacher daughter, Heather, being interviewed for some overseas radio programme. (I remember, also, that she acquitted herself very well, despite her father hopping round like an agitated hen in the background).

But these were all peripheral matters which were of little real consequence to any of us worshippers either at the time or in retrospect. What mattered most was that we were gathered together there to welcome and to celebrate Easter morning. And so we waited in the unrelieved darkness, in an attitude of almost breathless anticipation, for the sun to rise over Calvary before our very eyes on Easter Day.

Suddenly, almost without warning, it did just that. And as the sun rose with the swiftness typical of that part of the world and enveloped the site of Calvary and the Resurrection in golden light the then minister of St Andrew's, Rev Bill Gardiner Scott, called out, 'The Lord is risen' and the rest of us affirmed in response, 'The Lord is risen indeed'.

I doubt if any one of us had ever felt more sure of the Lord's resurrection than at that moment.

The Scots have their own church in Jerusalem, but the English have a Cathedral, St George's. The Anglican bishopric in Jerusalem was set up by Act of Parliament in 1841 and the first bishop took up residence in the following year. He began to build a church in the Old City near to Jaffa Gate. This was Christ Church. Completed in 1849, it was the Anglican Church in Jerusalem for half a century, but towards the end of the century work was begun on what was to become the magnificent structure we know now as St George's Cathedral. It was nearly twenty years in building but was completed in 1910.

A splendid building in its own right, St George's has a number of features in its interior that make it all the more pleasing to the visitor's eye. Its kneelers, the gift of parishes and individuals in England, are exquisitely embroidered; and the new organ, installed in 1984, is an extremely fine instrument. The Cathedral garden is an entrancing surprise to the first-time visitor. It is for all the world as if a typical English garden, well-stocked with flowers and plants of many descriptions, had been somehow transported into Jerusalem. Its sights and scents are a real joy.

On a Sunday morning in Jerusalem I worship in St Andrew's and there are always a fair number of my group who choose to worship there, too. Nearly always, there are also a number who choose to attend St George's. Since the St Andrew's service precedes St George's by an hour, I contrive to get something like the best of both worlds for the Presbyterians, including those who may be Presbyterians only for the day. I get the bus to take us over to St George's in time for the closing ten minutes or so of the service there. This allows us to stand at the back of the church and enjoy the final praise and closing organ music. This, plus a stroll round the garden, is a very satisfying end to the morning.

Jerusalem has, of course, many more Scottish and English connections than their churches provide or than have so far been mentioned; and a large number of these stretch far back into history. But there is one Scottish connection of modern times that I was personally a part instrument in making - although admittedly it is of a trivial nature. It happened in 1975. A few weeks before the starting date of my tour that year I received a letter from Joseph Aweidah, our tour agent in Jerusalem, asking if I could possibly be of assistance to his Jerusalem YMCA football team. Their football strip of scarlet and white required to be replaced but their former suppliers in Britain had ceased production; and he was writing to ask if his good friend Jim Martin might be able to procure a set of scarlet and white football jerseys and bring them out with him.

I was far from sure that I could but such a *cri de coeur* was not easy to ignore. So enquiries were made, the Sunday Post published the story; and the jerseys were obtained. A Motherwell firm of sportswear manufacturers - Top Mill - came up trumps. Having read in the press of my quest, they telephoned me and offered to supply jerseys in the colours desired. When I went to the factory and collected them, they refused to accept any payment. This, they insisted, was to be a gift in the cause of international friendship. And so, with the willing help of a few members of the group, the football jerseys were transported from Motherwell to Jerusalem and were received there with great delight, perhaps doing a little to foster Jerusalem-Scottish friendship.

There is no 'perhaps' whatsoever about the contribution made by St Andrew's Church and Hospice to such friendship. That this contribution has been substantial is a fact beyond dispute. One illustration of it which a group of mine was privileged to witness and even to participate in was the St Andrew's Day service of 1987. We were having a short (ten-day) pilgrimage of Church of Scotland people and the focal point of the tour was spending St Andrewstide in Jerusalem, living in the Scottish Hospice, joining in the St Andrew's Night Ceilidh and sharing in the annual St Andrew's Day service in St Andrew's Church on 30th November. On that St Andrew's night act of worship we were part of a congregation that packed the church with representatives of an astonishing number of Christian denominations. Our reflection that Jerusalem must surely contain more churches of different denominations than any other city in the world was swiftly engulfed by our exhilaration at being part of such a wide-ranging ecumenical gathering, with the clergy resplendent in their multifarious colours of vestment.

Peaceful and joyful though the scene was in the church that night, this same Scottish Church of St Andrew was once the very centre of furious crossfire from opposing armies. In the days of the partition after the British Mandate, St Andrew's was situated almost directly on the Israeli-Jordan border, just within the Israeli line and with an Arab Legion military post only yards away on the other side. When the Six Days' War erupted in all its fury in the summer of 1967, fierce fighting took place at this very spot and being in such a vulnerable position between the Israeli and the Arab guns, it was almost inevitable that the church should sustain severe damage. While all this was happening, the minister of the church, whose manse was adjacent to the church, was not at home. He was out doing some pastoral visiting in the city of Jerusalem and suddenly found himself caught up in the middle of some bitter street fighting. At first he had no alternative but to take what cover he could in the shelter of a doorway but after a time he managed, through skipping hastily from shelter to shelter, to make his way home, to be met on the one hand by the relief of his anxious wife and on the other by the sad sight of his beloved church pitted with shell holes.

That was one of the more painful of the dramatic experiences that have befallen the Church of Scotland in Jerusalem. Another of its episodes that was much more joyful but also had its element of drama concerned an old retainer. His home was near Bethlehem, in that area of the country popularly referred to today as the West Bank; and as a result he found that the partition settlement of 1948 cut him off completely from St Andrew's Hospice and his employment there. He had travelled back and forwards daily from his home to his duties but when the settlement was made and the border lines rigidly drawn, he was no longer able to make that journey. He and his job were now in separate countries and no commuting was possible between one and the other.

For nineteen years he was not able even to visit for a day the Hospice he had faithfully served. Came the Six Days' War in 1967 and the bursting asunder of the border restrictions in the Jerusalem area. Early the next morning the warden of St Andrew's Hospice answered a ring on the front door bell to find their old retainer standing there ready to begin his day's work - for all the world as if he had simply been away for the weekend and not for nineteen years.

Scotland and England have centuries old connections with the Holy City and nowhere perhaps is that connection given a more touching reminder

67

than in the British War Cemetery. Lying high up on Mount Scopus it commands a spectacular view over the whole of Jerusalem. There in their neat rows, rendered all the more moving because of the military precision of their serried ranks, are the last resting places of the many hundreds of Scots and English and other nationalities, too, who paid the supreme sacrifice in the liberation of Jerusalem in 1917.

Here my personal pilgrimage is once more intermingled with the memory of my brother killed in action, not in Palestine but in Germany. There was a day when I visited his grave and that day returns to me whenever I visit the War Cemetery on Mount Scopus.

I have often been to Becklingen in my mind but this time it was for real. Killed at the little village of Bleckede on the River Elbe, in the Battalion's last action of the war, George was buried, along with the other eighteen of his company who fell there, in the village cemetery but was later reinterred in a more permanent resting place in the massive and majestic British War Cemetery at Becklingen near Saltau on the edge of Luneberg Heath.

The day I went there was the first time I had ever seen a War Cemetery and I was awed and overwhelmed when I saw those 2,500 graves it contains, each one marked out with its white headstone and with the Cross of Sacrifice overlooking them all. Despite the helpfully detailed book of reference available, it took me some time to find the grave I wanted amongst that vast throng, but eventually I did. As I stood before it and read its inscription 'Rifleman George K. Martin. Killed in action 21 April 1945. Aged 21 years', I could not hold back the tears.

As the tears eased and I could see clearly again, I read the inscription on a neighbouring grave 'A solider of the war. Known to God' and the tears came again. Just then a voice spoke behind me in a broad Scottish accent, 'Is it someone of your own?' It was the caretaker of the cemetery, a Glaswegian, a solider who had married a German girl and settled in the once enemy land. And as I nodded dumbly in reply to his question, yet again the tears flowed. Weatherwise that was a grey day but every time I have gone to the War Cemetery on Mount Scopus it has been in the warm sunshine of early morning, a circumstance which seems only to accentuate its haunting poignancy. To stroll among those immaculately kept graves even for a few minutes in the morning sunshine in a land which has seen so much conflict and which sees so much still is somehow - paradoxically, no doubt - to be made to think also of the Prince of Peace who, just on the other side of the valley, himself made the greatest sacrifice the world has ever seen.

In the Environs of the Old City

$\mathbf{M}$ount Zion is today just outside the present walls of the Old City, which were built by Sultan Suleiman in 1517 at the beginning of the four centuries long Turkish occupation of Jerusalem. In ancient times, however, as might be expected, Mount Zion was inside the city walls and on Mount Zion there are several buildings of considerable interest to the tourist.

Here is situated, for example, what Jews have venerated from the twelfth century as the Tomb of King David. Few nowadays believe that the great monarch is actually buried here but his mausoleum is still one of the most revered places in the whole country.

Immediately above King David's Tomb - in the upper storey of the same building - is a place that is the object of somewhat similar veneration on the part of Christians. It is the traditional Room of the Last Supper. Usually referred to as the Cenacle (from the Latin *coenaculum* meaning 'dining hall'), it cannot, of course, be the actual room in which the Last Supper took place. The fact that the city has been destroyed and rebuilt since then makes that impossible. But it may well be that it took place on this site or very near at hand; and from early times Christians have visited here in commemoration of the event.

The Cenacle is a large, bare room with marked evidence all around of its past use both as a Moslem and as a Christian place of worship. Its bareness may come as a surprise to some. It certainly did to a twelve-year-old schoolboy from Glasgow during my first ever visit there. When he came into the room and looked around, he exclaimed in some surprise, 'But there isn't even a table.'

Our visit to the Cenacle is usually made all the more interesting because of its situation directly above the Tomb of King David. Always I have brief devotions in the Cenacle with my group - a reading, a prayer and a hymn -

and quite often the sound of our Christian devotions will mingle with the sound of the Jewish devotions that are proceeding in the room below, just a stair's depth away from us.

There was one occasion when our visit to these holy places was inadvertently the cause of an unholy row. In a way it was really all my fault. Rather absentmindedly I had taken the group to Mount Zion on a Friday afternoon, the eve of Sabbath. Most westerners are aware that the Jewish Sabbath falls on Saturday but it is not always easy to remember that the Jewish day runs not from midnight to midnight but from evening to evening. Officially it used to be that the day was over once three stars had appeared in the sky but long ago this was formalised to 6 pm. As a result, Sabbath commences at 6 pm on Friday evening and for practical purposes, because of the necessity to make preparations for the Sabbath, this has long meant that in many respects Sabbath cessation of activities begins on the Friday afternoon. Jewish shops, for instance, which may normally close for lunch at 1 pm to reopen at 4 pm will simply not open up again after the Friday lunch closure.

On this particular Friday afternoon I arrived with my group on Mount Zion to discover to my chagrin that not only was David's Tomb closed to visitors but so was the Room of the Last Supper. It was a severe disappointment that, in particular, the Cenacle was barred to us and so when a Jew approached me with a manner that carried the appearance of authority and made me an offer of help, I was exceeding vulnerable to a plausible tale.

'I am in charge here', he said 'And although the Upper Room is officially closed, I am permitted to admit visitors like yourselves but you will have to pay me for doing so.'

At that point another Jew interrupted. We did not know where he had come from - perhaps he just happened to be within earshot - but he called out, 'Do not listen to him. You do not need to pay him. I can get you in for nothing.'

'No, you can't', protested the first man. 'It is against the law for them to visit the Upper Room on the Sabbath. It can only be done by special arrangement through me and payment must be made for the privilege.'

'Don't listen to him,' the other insisted, 'He is not telling the truth and just wants to make some money.'

They began to expostulate with each other in Hebrew and in increasingly loud and angry tones. I cannot tell you who won the argument, if either of them did, for in the middle of their altercation we thought it prudent to steal quietly away and return another day to make our visit to the Cenacle.

Also on Mount Zion, and only some fifty yards walk from the Cenacle, is Dormition Abbey. This is an imposing church, with a number of beautiful mosaics, which houses in its crypt a stone effigy of St Mary asleep on her deathbed. *Dormire* is the Latin verb 'to sleep' and Dormitiron Abbey was built to pay homage to the Roman Catholic belief that upon her death Mary was taken into heaven body and soul.

I visited this place for the first time on Christmas Eve 1964 and I can still remember well the strange feeling that gripped me - a mixture of excitement and apprehension - as our party swung round the corner of the alley leading to the church. Staring us straight in the face, just ten yards beyond the entrance to the church, was a closed gate, heavily festooned with barbed wire and bearing a sign that said in large letters, 'It is dangerous to go further. No Man's Land'.

The church stood on the very edge of the partition between Israel and Jordan, and it accorded ill with our thoughts of the near approach of Christmas to see this warning and to see also the heavily armed soldiers on duty on the church tower.

I think of that every time I revisit Dormition Abbey, and sometimes mention it to my group. But no such sombre recollections happen along to lessen the pleasantness of the stroll down the hill as far as the Church of St Peter en Gallicantu (St Peter of the Cockcrow) which nestles against the hillside below Mount Zion. This modern church, built like so many Holy Land churches on the ruins of much earlier ones, is believed by many to stand where once stood the Palace of Caiaphas the High Priest.

It is notable for its mosaics. There is a striking mosaic fronting the Valley of Siloam which the church overhangs. Inside the church a series of equally striking mosaics adorns the walls and tells the story of Jesus arrested and on trial, and of Peter's denial. But what makes them unique - and singularly interesting to every visitor - is that they were the life's work of a single priest of the French Assumptionist order whose church it is.

Underneath the sanctuary is an area that may have been the courtyard of Caiaphas's palace, with galleries and staircases around it. I ask my groups to linger here for a space to try to visualise Peter warming himself at a brazier, having denied three times any knowledge of Jesus, when suddenly the cock crows and, at the same moment, Jesus, being led along one of the galleries above, catches Peter's eye.

Beneath the courtyard area is a bottle-type dungeon where, it is thought, Jesus may have been incarcerated for whatever remained part of the night after his trial before the Sanhedrin. Overlooking the dungeon is a guard room with a whipping-block for prisoners' punishment and staples all round the walls for prisoners' chains. There are visual aids in plenty for an attempt to project our imaginations backwards through the centuries.

On one occasion the drama we experienced in the guard room was not imaginary but only too real, and not of the past but very much of the present. We sat round the wall of the guard room while I pointed out its various features. Suddenly Roddy Devon slumped to the floor, his face ashen.

Although in his seventies, Roddy was a very fit man. A lifelong member of Motherwell Harriers, his hometown, he still ran regularly and even competitively. Yet here he was - without warning - unconscious and looking very poorly. Another member of my group that year was a retired hospital matron. When she examined Roddy, she said to me, 'He's a very ill man. You must get help at once'.

I rushed upstairs, out of the church and up more stairs to the priests' house opposite. Unfortunately, the priest I knew best and who spoke English fairly fluently was out and the priests there spoke no more English than I spoke French. Eventually, however, I managed to convey to them the urgency of the situation and they showed me to the telephone. I had barely succeeded in having the hospital emergency service summoned and still had the telephone in my hand, when a young Anglican priest from my group appeared at my side.

'I'm afraid it's too late', he said, 'He's gone. The matron says he has just died.'

My heart sank. I felt crushed and desperately sad - for Roddy, a friend of my own of long standing, for his wife and family back home, for the rest of the group. But the emergency squad was already on the way and I hurried outside to await their arrival. They were on the spot in next to no time, a handful of young medics with all sorts of modern equipment - and they were tremendous.

'I'm afraid he's already dead', I said to the young doctor in charge.

'Bring all the equipment down anyway', she commanded her team and down to the guard room went everyone and everything. What followed was to me an illuminating demonstration of high level efficiency in operation; and I enjoyed the demonstration all the more - in retrospect anyway - because it had a happy outcome. They ascertained that the retired matron's diagnosis had been premature. Roddy was still alive although unconscious. They attended to him there and then, transported him to the hospital and two days later he was restored to us fit and well. What had appeared to be a fatal heart attack turned out to be no more serious than a spectacular and frightening faint, occasioned, it was thought, by the press of bodies in the confined space of the underground guardroom.

I experienced drama of a different nature but in its own way just as severe a drain on my nervous energy in the course of my first visit to Mount Zion after the Six Days' War.

In the Environs of the Old City

For some reason I was not able to begin with Bethlehem as I usually do. Instead I took the group to Mount Zion on the morning after arrival. The initial tour is always a somewhat tense affair for the leader so far as 'shepherding his flock' is concerned, since he has not yet had time to get to know them well enough to be aware of any characteristics or tendencies that might need special attention or even special watchfulness.

On this occasion I found that I had not been sufficiently watchful with regard to John Smart. John was a very keen and a very able photographer, and as a result was naturally anxious to obtain as many good camera shots as he could.

It had been impressed on the group how important it was, vital even, that we should keep together and that no one should wander off on his or her own. John Smart had apparently taken these words of advice very seriously. On Mount Zion we had visited Dormition Abbey, King David's Tomb and the Cenacle and were about to pay a short visit to the small Holocaust Memorial which is also there. It was only then that John who, like the others, had faithfully remained close to the group, asked if he could miss out on the Holocaust visit so that he might go back and take a few more photographs at Dormition Abbey. He assured us that he already knew exactly what were the photographs he intended to take and where he was going to take them. He assured us, too, that he was perfectly clear as to the way there and back, only a couple of minutes' walk in fact; and that he would return to the precise spot where we now were in no more than fifteen minutes' time and would be waiting for us there when we emerged from the Memorial.

As you may well have guessed, John Smart was *not* there when we returned to our rendezvous spot in some twenty minutes' time. A little disappointed that he had not kept his so firmly made promise about the time he would be away and also a little bit worried about the delay in what was . rather a tightly scheduled programme, we nevertheless waited as patiently as we were able. Only Mrs Smart expressed any annoyance at his being late - 'Typical', she snorted, 'He loses all sense of time and place when he's taking photographs'. When, however, a further ten minutes passed and he still had not appeared, her irritation changed to anxiety and we all became concerned.

We organised a systematic search for him. Leaving a few at what was to have been our meeting point, the rest of us split up and combed the not very large area thoroughly but failed to find him. We went over the whole area once more, more painstakingly and even more systematically, but still we found no trace of him. By now it was almost an hour after our agreed time of meeting with him and the leader was in a state of distress almost matching that of Mrs Smart. Where could he have gone? What could have happened?

Travels in the Holy Land

Had he taken ill? Was he perhaps even now in hospital - had some other kind of disaster overtaken him? Imagine losing one of my group. I felt awful.

Common sense attempted to take over. 'Nothing harmful can have happened. He has simply got confused, lost his way and wandered off Mount Zion altogether. He has probably made his way back to the hotel by now. We'll find him there when we go back for lunch.' By this stage I was beyond taking any comfort from such attempted rationalisation, utterly sensible though it undoubtedly was. I would be reassured only when I actually saw him safe and well.

It was, therefore, with apprehension as well as hope that I returned at last with the others to the hotel. And John Smart was not there. This threw me into the depths of despair and John's poor wife was brokenhearted. There seemed nothing else for it now but to enlist the help of the police. Before doing that, however, I felt for some reason that I ought to go back to Mount Zion myself and have one final look to satisfy myself that he was not there. It seemed an extremely forlorn hope but we called a taxi and a few of us returned to Mount Zion. Wonder of wonders, there was John Smart, standing almost precisely on the spot where we had arranged to meet him - and a very angry John Smart it was.

He was positively irate - irate at the group, and particularly at the leader, for having, as he put it, abandoned him. He maintained that, although he had kept the rendezvous both with regard to time and place, he had not seen any sign of us. He had been forced to spend the best part of two hours exposed to the heat and the dust, pacing up and down, waiting in vain for us to turn up (and all the while growing more and more angry). He had had no alternative, he grumbled, except to wait and wait because he could not remember the name of the hotel we were staying in, far less how to find it.

Every effort on our part to tell him that in fact the group had returned to the appointed place at the appointed time and had spent a considerable time searching the area thereafter was just swept aside. He simply would not accept that version of events. It could not possibly be true because *he* had not deviated one iota from the agreed plan and, therefore, there was absolutely no doubt that the fault lay with the rest of the group, and the leader in particular who should have ensured that the arrangement was adhered to. Somehow or other he had been abandoned callously and unfeelingly, a stranger in a strange land, and he felt very, very sore about it.

Nothing was ever able to shake him from that conviction, even when we found him speaking about buildings that he could not possibly have seen unless he had moved a considerable distance from where he was supposed to have been. This was, nevertheless, sufficient to ease my conscience and relieve my fears that perhaps I had somehow been inefficient in the manner

74

of the search for him. The truth of the matter clearly was that in the unfamiliarity of the environment he had become disorientated without ever having the faintest inkling of the fact; and had wandered off Mount Zion altogether. How he ever succeeded in finding his way back to the appointed place of meeting I will never understand. But I was most relieved that he did.

I was also greatly relieved when, a few years later, Mr and Mrs Smart came again with me on a Holy Land pilgrimage. I took from that that in the end he could not have reckoned me all that bad a leader.

From Gallicantu we usually walk further down the hillside into the Valley of Siloam (or Silwan) and to the Pool of Siloam. Many visitors are terribly disappointed when they are given their first sight of this. The popular hymn 'By cool Siloam's shady rill' has led them to expect to see something in the nature of a sparkling pool of clear water in a sylvan setting. Instead they come upon a body of dull-looking water enclosed in concrete at the foot of a flight of stone steps where the distance below ground level effectively shuts out most of the sunlight.

Things are not, however, nearly so unattractive or uninteresting as they first appear. The Pool of Siloam empties into a stream which flows on down the valley and amongst the trees - not quite, perhaps, the same as the picture conjured up by the 'shady rill' of the hymn but much nearer to it.

The really fascinating feature about the Pool of Siloam is where it comes from. It is the other end of a tunnel leading from a spring further up the Valley of Siloam; and the story of this tunnel is one of the great epics of Old Testament times.

In 701 BC Hezekiah was King in Jerusalem and the Assyrians under Sennacherib were about to lay siege to the city. The city's water supply was particularly vulnerable to any siege situation, since it was dependent on a single spring (Gihon, a name which means 'gushing') located outside the city walls in the Siloam valley.

Hezekiah decided that there would be no real hope of successfully resisting the impending siege unless some means was devised of safeguarding the city's water supply. His plan was to have a tunnel cut through the rock so that the water might flow underground from Gihon to an artificially constructed pool inside the city walls - what was to become the Pool of Siloam - while at the same time camouflaging the Gihon spring so that the besieging enemy would not locate it.

Accordingly, he set two groups of engineers to work cutting the tunnel, and in great haste. One set started their operation from Gihon and the other from Siloam with the intention of meeting in the middle. Their goal was accomplished, not only speedily but with very little deviation of course being required in order to achieve the meeting together of the two halves of the tunnel. When we take into account the date of this enterprise and all that the engineers were lacking therefore in terms of present day engineering technology and equipment; and when we take into account also the necessity for breakneck speed, as is clearly evidenced by the marks of their tools in the walls of the tunnel, the making of Hezekiah's Tunnel must rank as one of the great engineering feats of all time.

Hezekiah's Tunnel is 1749 feet (533 metres) long and is walkable provided you are prepared to wade along a watercourse that, even in summer, may reach waist-high in parts and are prepared also to walk at times bent double when the roof of the tunnel descends so low as to require that posture. Many tourists do walk the tunnel. It is most commonly done from the Gihon end and, if time permits, it is an interesting and exciting adjunct to the tour. Clearly not to be recommended to anyone suffering from claustrophobia but otherwise well worth the time and effort involved.

By the time you have splashed your way slowly and carefully along the winding length of the tunnel, using your obligatory flashlight both to avoid painful contact with the tunnel walls and roof and also to observe the marks left on these walls and roof by the tools of the workers twenty-seven centuries ago, you will appreciate even more the marvellous feat the construction of the tunnel was.

We can read about it in the Old Testament: 1 Kings 1:45 and 2 Kings 20:20. But even more information is gleaned from an inscription in Hebrew that was engraved on the wall of the tunnel, no doubt by the engineer in charge, near to the exit into the Pool of Siloam. It reads: 'Behold the tunnel. This is the story of its cutting. While the miners swung their picks, one towards the other, and when there remained only 3 cubits to cut, the voice of one calling his fellow was heard - for there was a resonance in the rock coming from both north and south. So the day they broke through the miners struck, one against the other, pick against pick, and the waters flowed from the spring towards the pool, 1200 cubits. The height of the rock above the head of the miners was 100 cubits'.

This inscription was discovered by accident in 1880 and is now preserved in the Museum of the Ancient Orient in Istanbul.

Another 'exhibit' in the Jerusalem area that can transport our imagination far back into the past is King Solomon's Quarries. This is an enormous cavern that extends, from its entrance in the city walls between Herod's Gate and Damascus Gate, more than 200 yards underneath the streets of the Old City. It is believed that it was here that the stones were quarried for the building of Solomon's Temple.

Although I always endeavour to take my groups to Solomon's Quarries, this is not usually included in the official itinerary which means that transport is not provided for the visit. Frequently, therefore, in order to add some local colour, I have my group travel from our Panorama Hotel on the Jericho Road in the local Arab bus. On one occasion this provided a remarkable illustration of Arab friendliness to strangers.

I was standing at the stop with twenty-five members of my group when the bus came in sight,. I could see that already all the seats were occupied and that, in addition, some people were standing. 'How long will it be until the next bus, Hamid?' I asked, for he was accompanying us.

'Everyone will get on *this* bus', he replied.

'Impossible,' I protested, 'Look, there are already people standing.'

'I know, but we'll get on', Hamid insisted, 'You'll see.'

And see we certainly did. The bus was a 35-seater, single-decker. It halted at the stop and we waited for the exodus from it that I thought Hamid must be anticipating, but no one got off. Nevertheless, the driver waved us on – and every single one of us boarded that bus. What is more, most of the group even got seats, because all over the bus people were not only squeezing up but rising and insisting that the tourists should sit. It was, admittedly, a bit like a sardine tin - some 65 passengers in a 35-seater bus - but we all were taken on.

It was a remarkable experience and marvellous fun, not least after we had completed the descent past the Garden of Gethsemane and, crossing the Kedron, had begun the ascent on the other side of the valley. Here the rather ancient and grossly overloaded bus started to travel ever more slowly until even the pedestrians on the pavement were overtaking it. I thought it could not possibly make it to the top without some of us first getting out, but it did.

As we stroll around the massive vault of Solomon's Quarries and see so clearly the marks made by the ancient stone-cutters upon the white limestone walls and roof, the vivid accounts of the building of the Temple recorded in 1 Kings 5 and 6 and in Chronicles become even more vivid. How easily we can visualise the quarrying and the shaping of the stones being done there without any of the sounds being heard in the city streets just overhead ('there was neither hammer nor axe nor any tool of iron heard in the house while it was in building', 2 Kings 6:7).

Strewn all over the vast area of the cavern floor are fragments of the white limestone of all shapes and sizes, some of them undoubtedly left there by those Temple-building masons of long ago. Many tourists pick up some of these pieces to take home as souvenirs - or perhaps to give to a Freemason friend, for Freemasons hold Solomon's Quarries in great regard. The tradition is that the builders of the Temple were the first Freemasons; and pieces of stone from the Quarries are to be found all over the world, shaped into the form of masonic insignia.

Not far away from Solomon's Quarries - just across the road, in fact, and behind the bus station - is the Garden Tomb. This is what some believe, and many others would like to believe, is the true site of the crucifixion and resurrection of Jesus. It is a very pleasing and devotional site but it must be said that the traditional site of the Church of the Holy Sepulchre is most likely to be the authentic one.

The Garden Tomb is closely associated with General Gordon of Khartoum fame. There is a hill directly behind the bus station and closely adjacent to the Garden Tomb which Gordon identified in 1883 as Golgotha. His identification was partly based on the fact that the holes and depressions on the face of the hill may be observed to have a skull-like appearance. This, however, is a rather flimsy platform on which to build a theory since the contours of the hill may well have changed considerably over nineteen centuries. Moreover, while the New Testament speaks of the place of crucifixion as being the 'place of a skull', it does not say that this name derives from its appearance.

However, Gordon's claim prompted excavations in the near vicinity and when an early rolling stone type of tomb was discovered, that was taken by many to settle the issue. And so, for about a hundred years, an alternative site has been offered in Jerusalem to the rather unpleasing traditional site of the Church of the Holy Sepulchre.

The Garden Tomb site is beautiful and is wonderfully suited for remembering the story of the resurrection of Jesus. It is always a special source of inspiration for me personally to have my group sing there the triumphant Easter hymn, 'Thine be the glory, risen, conquering son'.

The Garden Tomb is not to be missed when you visit Jerusalem. I have conducted Communion services there for my groups in years past and one such particularly lives in my memory. It was towards the end of May 1967, just about two weeks before the outbreak of the Six Days' War, although we had at the time no inkling that that was imminent.

For this service we were greatly assisted by the kindness and courtesy of the Arab Christian caretaker, Mr Matta. He was an enormous help with all the necessary arrangements that led to our having a most uplifting Communion service in a superb setting. I returned to the Garden almost exactly a year later and found it little changed in itself. Some signs were still visible of the fierce fighting that had waged across it and around it but it was, nevertheless, much the same as I had seen it twelve months before, just as attractive and just as peaceful.

But Mr Matta was no longer there. He had been shot dead in the fighting, an innocent casualty of man's inhumanity to man. He was killed close by the holy place that he had tended so lovingly, the place which speaks so movingly of the death of Jesus. There was something surely poignantly fitting in that, for it was human sin that killed Jesus, too.

How Far is it to Bethlehem?

'How far is to Bethlehem?' asks the carol; and replies, 'Not very far'. That answer is capable of many interpretations, all of them significant. Taken literally, it is undoubtedly true of the distance in miles from Jerusalem - no more than half a dozen. And yet on my very first visit to the Holy Land those few miles might just as well have been hundreds so far as the accessibility of Bethlehem to us was concerned. It was on the occasion of the Dunera Educational Cruise to which I make reference elsewhere. Berthed in Haifa for two days, we made a day trip to Jerusalem on Christmas Eve. In those days, prior to the Six Days' War, the political separation between Israel and Jordan was rigid. Travel to Jordan from Israel and back again was impossible. As a result there was no way we could visit Bethlehem (in Jordan) from Haifa (in Israel) and return to the ship. One way travel only was the order of the day so far as the borders were concerned.

As for Bethlehem that day, the best that could be done for us was to take us to Ramat-Rahel, which means 'Height of Rachel'. This was a kibbutz set on a hilltop from which we were able to get a view of Bethlehem, still some distance away but the closest view possible from Israeli territory. Although we had left Haifa in bright sunshine, here it was raining steadily, which made our distant glimpse of Bethlehem even less clear than it would have been on a good day. Not only so, as we clustered in the rain on that vantage point, peering intently across the intervening rain-besmirched distance towards Bethlehem, we found ourselves first of all staring at machine-gun emplacements less than a hundred yards away; because, of course, we were right on the border between Israel and Jordan.

All the same, despite our distance from Bethlehem, despite the curtain of rain lessening the clarity of our vision, despite the proximity of weapons of war, it was for me - and, I know, not only for me - very moving to set eyes, even from so far away, on the town where Jesus was born. When, back on board ship that evening, we packed into Dunera's assembly hall for our Christmas Eve Watchnight Service, it was all the more meaningful because we had actually looked upon Bethlehem, so much so that we could almost hear the angels' singing and see the star in the sky.

Six months later these feelings were intensified when I actually visited Bethlehem and the Church of the Nativity which stands at its centre.

The town where Jesus was born must always have a special interest for any and every Christian; and for those who actually see it is likely to cause a tug at the heartstrings. It is no longer the 'little town' of the carol but has a population of some fifty thousand people. By far the most of these are Arabs and a great many of these are Christians, the majority of whom are Roman Catholic.

Bethlehem is a Hebrew name which means 'House of Bread' and, when you visit it, you can have no doubt that the birth of Jesus is at its heart. This, it must be said, is very much the case in the commercial sense.

The economy of Bethlehem in modern times depends very largely on the fact that it was the birthplace of Jesus. Tourism and its accessories constitute its chief and almost its only industry. Every year - at least when things are normal or near normal - thousands upon thousands of tourists flock to Bethlehem from all over the world simply because Jesus was born there. And its factories and shops are very heavily involved in the making and the selling of souvenirs of a Christian, and particularly of a Christmas, character.

One souvenir product which many find very attractive are their olive wood figures, especially the hand-carved ones. My wife is convinced that I suffer from a kind of addiction here as I bring back a few from every trip I make. I do find them most appealing, not only because of their appearance but also because they come from olive trees that grew in the Bethlehem area and because they are carved in the town itself.

Mark you, it is not a matter of cutting down an olive tree and immediately setting to work on carving figures out of the wood. Olive wood has to lie for at least two years, preferably three, before it is ready to be worked on. Then it is fashioned into a multitude of figures - donkeys and camels and 'good shepherds' (shepherds with a lamb on their shoulders or at their side) and a whole lot more. Personally I am very fond of the good shepherd kind of carving but pride of place in my affections - as with many pilgrims - is given to the olive wood nativity scenes which come in all sizes (and prices). These usually consist of fourteen figures - three wise men, two shepherds, three sheep, three oxen, and, of course, Mary, Joseph and the baby Jesus lying in his crib.

Until the *intifada* began at the end of 1987, I used to arrange for my group to have an evening excursion to Bethlehem for the purpose of shopping. This arrangement was made with a twofold purpose in mind. For one thing it avoided having our daytime itinerary interrupted by too many or too prolonged shopping stops. For another thing, it allowed for shopping (which nearly every tourist feels is a must in greater or less degree) to be carried out in a more leisurely and satisfying manner than could ever be possible in the midst of an afternoon or morning tour. Most important of all, perhaps, it enabled the group to have an outing (at no extra cost) from Jerusalem to Bethlehem under a starlit evening sky and to have the run of an attractive store all to themselves for an hour or two.

Most group members down the years have felt that such a nocturnal trip was a very worthwhile experience, a judgment which had little to do with whether many or few purchases were made, if any. The significant fact was that the outing was to Bethlehem and Bethlehem was the place where Jesus had been born. It was that same fact which added a special dimension to the time when, instead of being accommodated as usual in a Jerusalem hotel, we were put up for a week in a hotel in Bethlehem. Bethlehem is much less convenient than Jerusalem as a starting point for most of our tours; but there was some compensation in actually living for a brief space in the very town where Jesus had been born.

It was during our stay there that I, to my considerable embarrassment, found myself locked out of my hotel. It is the practice for most tour leaders to use the services of a guide for part of the Jerusalem area period. On this occasion I had, as often, Hamid Essayad as that guide. The previous year I had used Ribhi Assuli; and I regarded both as personal friends. One night, towards the close of our week in Bethlehem, they came together to the hotel so that they might escort me round Bethlehem at night, finishing with a snack in a late-night cafe. When they brought me back to the hotel, I was to find it all locked up and the foyer in darkness. It was not really very late - before midnight in fact - but it was a small hotel, and, thinking all the guests had gone to bed, they had locked up and gone to bed themselves.

It was in that same Bethlehem hotel that John Sergeant's sultana cake did the disappearing trick. He had learned from previous visits the helpfulness of bringing out with him something edible to accompany the late evening cup of tea most of us Scots insisted on having before retiring. Being a dab hand at baking, he decided to give his friends a treat and baked a large sultana cake which he brought out with him, unknown to the rest of us.

On our first evening in Bethlehem, some had retired for an early night and the rest had gathered in the hotel lounge to have a pre-bedtime cuppa. When the tea was served, John said, 'Hold on a minute', went to his room and returned to reveal the mouth-watering sight of his home-baked sultana cake.

As he proceeded to cut a slice of his cake for each of the tea party, the hotel's owner-manager came along to enquire if all was well. John offered him too a piece of his cake. He enjoyed it so much that he was moved to say, 'I've never tasted anything so good. May I take your beautiful cake to show to my wife and family, who also live in the hotel?'

'Of course', said John, more than a little pleased at such warm interest being shown in his creation. 'Here, take the cake through to them and let them have a-piece each.' Off went Mr Handal with John's cake while we polished off our pieces with great relish and looked forward with considerable pleasure to another instalment of the same the following night.

Alas, that was not to be. Whether it was a case of misunderstanding John Sergeant's intention or a case of the excellence of his cake proving too big a temptation to the Handal family, the sad fact from our point of view was that we never saw any of that beautiful cake again. The Handal family (aided by the hotel staff?) consumed it all.

Another disappointment of this nature with a marked Bethlehem connection occured one Christmas Day back home. Let me explain.

The area round Hebron, some ten miles south of Bethlehem, is one of the most luxuriant vine-growing areas in the world. The grapes are luscious and abundant. One of the minor ironies of the Holy Land is met here. The Moslems who grow and harvest the grapes in the Hebron district are forbidden alcohol by their religion and consequently their grapes are transported to Bethlehem where the Christians make large quantities of wine out of them.

Although none of us was in any way a connoisseur of wine nor even competent to judge whether the Bethlehem wine was even of a reasonable quality, we found it quite enjoyable to have a glass with our dinner some nights, especially in that geographical context and knowing its local origin. Some of us had the brilliant idea of taking some wine home with us so that, come Christmas Day, we might drink a glass of wine made in Bethlehem on the birthday of the Baby born there to become the Saviour of the world.

Came Christmas Day, and with it the never-failing wonder and joy of the Christmas worship. Then the family gathering and the Christmas dinner - and the wine brought all the way from Bethlehem. I was quite excited as I opened the bottle and poured the wine - and it was awful. Perhaps it had tasted better in the Holy Land itself because we were there or perhaps it did not carry well. At any rate, I never again brought any home.

The birth of Jesus, it is true, is at the heart of Bethlehem in the commercial sense. It is also true in the geographical sense for right in the middle of the town, in what is called Manger Square, stands the Church of the Nativity, built over the birthplace of Jesus. This is the oldest place of Christian worship in the world. There has been an unbroken history of Christian worship here ever since the Emperor Constantine built the church in 326 AD.

Travels in the Holy Land

His mother, Queen Helena, whose devotion and research were the means of identifying many Christian sites - the Church of the Holy Sepulchre among them - had satisfied herself that she had located the site of Jesus' birth. At her request, Constantine had a church built over the cave which Christians had been venerating for the past two centuries as the birthplace and whose sanctity Hadrian had attempted to defile by putting a Temple of Venus on top of it.

Since it was first built, the church has suffered many changes and quite a lot of damage. In the sixth century it was rebuilt and enlarged by the Emperor Justinian. In the twelfth century it was completely restored by the Crusaders. Nevertheless, it may well still be spoken of as Constantine's church; and not a little of the original church is there to be seen to this day.

Inside the church several trapdoors are to be found set in the stone floor. Raise one of these and you will see below you part of the mosaic flooring of the original church, its colours still astonishingly fresh even after 1600 years. The outer walls of the first church are still in use and the four parallel rows, each of twelve red limestone pillars, in the interior, probably stood in the original church, too. These pillars display to this day figures of saints painted on them by Crusaders all of 800 years ago.

The main focus of interest for the Christian pilgrim is, however, not to be found in the church but below it. Flights of steps on either side of the altar lead down to two small caves, side by side. One is the Grotto of the Manger where, according to tradition, the infant Jesus was laid and the other is the Grotto of the Nativity where he was born.

A silver star set in marble at one end of the Grotto of the Nativity marks the traditional site of the birth. No one, of course, can say with any certainty that it was exactly here or there that the birth took place but I for one am in no doubt that it was at least hereabouts. Not that it matters very much. As I regularly say to my groups before we sing a Christmas hymn, read part of the Christmas story from the Bible and join in a short prayer, what does matter is the sure fact that Jesus *was* born. Wherever precisely the birth may have occurred, the baby born in Bethlehem whose nativity is commemorated by the Church of the Nativity in Manger Square has made a tremendous difference to the world and to countless thousands of its people.

I have visited the Church of the Nativity many times but I never fail to be deeply moved every time I descend to the Grotto of the Nativity. I know, too, that it is similar with most Christian pilgrims. There was one instance, for example, when we were spending the first morning of our pilgrimage in Bethlehem. After spending some time in the church above, I led the group down the steps into the Church of the Nativity. We had it all to ourselves for a space and I followed my usual pattern of a few words of explanation and comment, then our brief devotions, concluding with 'O come, all ye faithful'.

How Far is it to Bethlehem?

As I shepherded the group up the stairs back to the church above, Jenny Morrison came alongside me and whispered, 'Supposing I were to see nothing else, it has been well worthwhile coming to the Holy Land just for this'.

I did not look too closely and the light was dim just there, but I was sure there were tears in her eyes as she spoke. There was certainly no doubt at all about the tears - not only in the eyes but also streaming down the faces - of the party of Finns who followed us into the Grotto on another occasion.

As we were coming to the close of our brief devotional service beside the silver star, this group of some forty to fifty people gathered on the stairs leading down into the Grotto. They waited there in quiet reverence until we were finished. Then, as I began to usher my people up the stairs on the other side, they simultaneously began to descend. As they did so, they started to sing in Finnish the carol, 'Still the Night', and I could see on practically every face a cascade of tears. Those of us who had not yet moved out of the Grotto joined in the carol in English and found that, despite ourselves, we were joining in with our tears as well.

It can also be an emotional experience when we visit the Field of the Shepherds close beside Bethlehem. The Shepherds' Field is not, as we might expect, a single field or even a group of fields marked off in the British manner by fences or hedges or some such dividing agency. The Shepherds' Field is, in fact, an extensive area of pasture land running along the valley lying below the hill on which Bethlehem is built.

There is, of course, no way of knowing which particular section of this area best deserves to be designated *the* Field of the Shepherds, the actual location of the angels' message to the 'humble shepherds watching their flocks in Bethlehem's plains' at the first Christmas. It is scarcely surprising, therefore, that there are no less than three separate sites which have each been termed the Field of the Shepherds.

The Greek Orthodox site includes a natural cave which as long ago as the fourth century was given a mosaic floor. Not long afterwards the cave was cut open so that it was made possible to build a church within it. The new church standing there today was erected in 1955. This is a very popular site, much frequented by pilgrim groups. Not nearly so much frequented is the Protestant or YMCA site, perhaps because there is so little there in the way of church buildings, either ancient or modern; but its very simplicity and lack of adornment endear it to many.

The one which I tend to favour, all things considered, is the Roman Catholic site. Even when sites have little claim to precise historical accuracy, they may still be of considerable potential helpfulness to the pilgrim in terms of commemoration of something significant, a sort of visual aid, if you like. This is so of all three Shepherds' Fields and not least in this regard, in my

Travels in the Holy Land

view, is the Roman Catholic one.

For one thing, it provides a good vantage point for looking across the whole expanse of the string of fields which bear the name. For another thing, we see the remains of the Byzantine Church which once stood here, showing that in all probability this was a venerated spot as far back as the fourth century. Then there is the cave close to the ruins which, if it did not ever provide shelter and rest for the shepherds of the Christmas story, must be very similar to those that did. Now fashioned into a simple little chapel where we may pause for a few minutes to pray and reflect, its smoke-blackened roof bears testimony to many centuries of human use. And immediately above the cave is the Church of the Angel whose strikingly beautiful murals rehearse eloquently the story of the shepherds and the 'glad tidings of great joy' which came to them.

The commemorative quality of all three sites is enhanced by the fact that they are adjacent to the village of Beit Sahur which means literally 'the house of the nightwatching'. The very name is evocative of the Gospel narrative of the first Christmas. It was in this area that shepherds in the time of Jesus, as the general practice was, gathered their separate flocks into one large flock for the hours of darkness. By so doing they were able to take it in turns to eat and to sleep in one of the nearby caves - similar to the one we find on view - while the others looked after the sheep. In the morning the flocks were ever so easily split into their separate units. The shepherds simply stood one after another on a convenient rock or hillock and called out to their sheep. The sheep all knew their own shepherd's voice and responded to it; and very soon the various flocks were heading to the area of pasture that had been agreed on round the camp-fire the night before.

The almost personal relationship that existed between a good shepherd and his sheep, of which the New Testament speaks more than once, was a necessary ingredient of this operation. That sort of relationship is still in evidence today. I have observed it myself.

One year, when I took my group to the Field of the Shepherds and first of all to the Byzantine church remains, there was a shepherd with his flock of sheep in the field, quite close to where we stopped for my explanation and comment. Just as I finished what I had to say, almost as if it had been prearranged, the shepherd apparently decided it was time to move to a new location. He rose from where he had been sitting in the shade of a tree and climbed on top of a boulder some yards away. From there he began to call out names one after another. Each time he called out a name, one of the grazing sheep lifted its head and trotted over to his side. When he had collected all of them around him, he came down from the boulder and led them across the field to a fresh pasture.

86

That shepherd clearly knew his sheep by name and cared for them individually; and they knew and trusted him. And so once again in the Holy Land the Bible came alive for us.

The Lowest Spot on the Earth's Surface

It is always an exciting part of any Holy Land trip to visit the Dead Sea for this is the lowest spot on the surface of the earth. The very journey to it is an enlightening adventure.

Nearly every Holy Land pilgrim will be familiar with the Parable of the Good Samaritan before he goes there; and most will remember well that it begins by telling of a traveller 'going down' from Jerusalem to Jericho. When they follow in that traveller's train some two thousand years later, they speedily discover the factual accuracy of that description.

It is a rapid and a steep descent from Jerusalem to Jericho. Jerusalem is some 2900 feet above sea-level while Jericho is 1300 feet below. The journey, therefore, involves a drop of well over four thousand feet in the space of less than twenty miles.

Even those who, like myself, have been making that descent over no greater a period than the last quarter of a century will in that comparatively short period have seen the road repeatedly modernised and straightened. But there is more than enough still visible of the previous roads to reveal how many sharp turns and narrow passes they had, providing ideal territory for thieves and robbers to lie in wait and ambush unfortunate and unwary travellers.

Banditry of this sort had made the road notorious before the time of Jesus and its notoriety continued well into the present century. Even when H.V. Morton was researching in the 1930s for his famous book on the Holy Land, he was warned about the dangers of travelling this road alone, even in a car:

> 'When I told a friend that I intended to 'run down' to the Dead Sea for a day, he said, 'Well, be careful to get back before dark.' 'Why?' I asked. 'You might meet Abu Jildah.' 'Who is Abu Jildah?' 'He is a brigand who has shot several policemen. There is a price of £250 on his head, and he

The Lowest Spot on the Earth's Surface

has a habit of building a wall of stones across the Jericho road, stopping cars, robbing you, and if you resist, shooting you. He once held up fourteen cars in a row on this road, robbed everyone, threatened to cut off a woman's finger because her rings were tight, and was off and away to the hills by the time the police heard about it. So take my tip and get back before dusk . . .'

H.V. Morton, *In The Steps of the Master* p85.

In fact the Jerusalem-Jericho road gained the nickname The Way of Blood because of the number of hold-ups and muggings it witnessed. Even speeding down today's modern version of the road in a modern bus, it is not at all difficult to imagine how it could lend itself in the old - and not so old - days to surprise attacks on unprepared travellers.

Such imagining serves to enhance rather than diminish the fascination felt as the descent to Jericho unveils through the windows of the bus a succession of interesting pictures - the characteristic black tents of the Bedouin encamped near the roadway, all sprouting television aerials and many with a Mercedes car parked next to the tent; the steadily increasing number of new Jewish settlements, all of them heavily fortified; the ancient shepherds' road to Bethlehem winding its way through the sparsely vegetated hills; the Inn of the Good Samaritan (of which more later); and once, to the delight of more than the matrons in the party, we stopped to inspect at the roadside a week-old camel with its mother in close attendance.

Jericho itself is a place full of fascination - all three of them. Yes, all three - Ancient Jericho, Herodian Jericho and Modern Jericho.

Ancient Jericho is the oldest city known to the world. Following on the excavations of Professor Garstang in the 1930s, Dame Kathleen Kenyon, the British archaeologist whose name and exploits are legendary in the Holy Land, uncovered a part of the city wall and a watch tower which have been established as going back to about 8000 BC, making them around 10,000 years old. To look upon these and to think of people living on this very spot in community all these centuries ago is supremely fascinating in itself. That fascination is increased when we look across and beyond Kathleen Kenyon's excavations. They have as their background a high escarpment which is known as the Mount of Temptation. Tradition has it that this was the scene of the conflict Jesus had with the Devil which is recorded in the gospels.

If we now make a complete about turn and look in the opposite direction, we find before us a scene of lush green growth which is in startling contrast to the forbidding, even frightening, barrenness of the surrounding wilderness. All this luxuriance is due to the irrigating bountifulness of the River Jordan, aided by the waters of Elisha's Spring. What we see is the same sort of breathtaking surprise sight that the Israelites under Moses' leadership looked upon from the other side of the Jordan after forty years of wandering in the wilderness. No wonder they recognised at once that they had come at last to the long awaited 'land flowing with milk and honey', the promised land.

Modern Jericho is close by the Tel of Ancient Jericho. The present day town is both large and busy. Its streets are vividly adorned in the touring season by bougainvillea and flame trees in particular, and rendered even more colourful by the fruit set out on display at a multitude of shops. We normally make a stop at one of these shops, usually after the rather hot and dusky trek up the Tel, to purchase some fruit and to enjoy a delectable drink of orange or grapefruit juice, freshly pressed in our presence.

All that is now to be seen of Herodian Jericho is to be found about two miles to the south of the modern town. Some time after the destruction of the ancient city, people began to live again on the site and cultivate things like balsam and dates and fruit. Later still Antony made a gift of these exotic gardens to Cleopatra who in turn rented them out to Herod the Great. Soon after this Herod, indefatigable builder that he was, decided to build a new town nearby but not too near the produce he had leased from Cleopatra. So he created there a Jericho of Roman character, with a winter palace, an amphitheatre and a hippodrome. Today we see only a mound and imagination must be enlisted to fill in the detail of what it all looked like in Herod's day.

Close by Jericho is that part of the River Jordan which tradition has marked as the place where Jesus was baptised by John the Baptist. This particular location has been inaccessible to pilgrims since the 1967 war and I have, therefore, been unable to visit it since then. I can still remember clearly, however, that it was with a feeling of some surprise, perhaps even tinged with disappointment, that I first saw it. At that point the Jordan is sluggish and brown, not the clear, fast-flowing river I had somehow been expecting to see.

Jericho lies a mile or two north of the Dead Sea. A mile or two south of the Dead Sea's northern end are the excavated ruins of the Qumran settlement. This was the home of the Essene community of the first century AD to whom we owe the now famous Dead Sea Scrolls.

It was in 1947 that the Scrolls were discovered - after having lain hidden and unsuspected in surrounding caves for nineteen centuries. An Arab, known as Mohammed the Wolf, who was goatherding in the area happened to throw a stone through the opening of one of the many caves that dotted the cliff face. He was astonished to hear the unmistakable sound of something breaking as the stone made impact with it inside the cave.

This led him to investigate. Inside the cave he found a number of tall earthenware jars with lids on top and he discovered that these jars contained old parchments wrapped in linen. He had no inkling of the nature, still less of the value, of what were later to be recognised as priceless manuscripts; but he was the one who set in motion the chain of events which uncovered them to the knowledge and to the inspection of the world.

Written out by members of the Essene community, some of the manuscripts are copies of Biblical (Old Testament) books, others are Essene manuals.

It took some time before someone recognised that what the goatherd had stumbled upon was of immense importance and value. But no sooner had that recognition been made than there began an intensive search of all the surrounding caves. Many of them yielded up further scrolls, eleven caves in particular. This, in turn, led to exploratory excavation on a site nearby where there were indications of early human occupation; and so it was that there were uncovered the remains of the monastery of the Essenes, the puritanistic sect who had put the scrolls in the cave for safe keeping against the imminent arrival of the Roman Army in 68 AD.

The discovery of the Dead Sea Scrolls and of the Essene monastery ruins is one of the most thrilling archaeological finds of this century; and it has provided Holy Land tourists with a marvellously exciting visit. Today it is a well-organised and well-appointed site with guiding signs and captions, wooden steps and stairs around the excavations, as well as a parking place, toilets and an airconditioned cafe closely adjacent to the site. But when I visited it for the first time in 1965 things were much different. The present modern road from Jericho south along the Dead Sea coast did not exist. Those of us who wanted to see Qumran had to make a bumpy taxi ride over what was no better than a rough track in order to get there.

We were not dismayed, however, as we reckoned it would be well worth enduring a little discomfort for the thrill of being able, as our guide assured us we would, actually to go inside Cave 4 where the majority of the most valuable scrolls had been retrieved. But when we reached the site, we found confronting us a barbed wire fence straddling the narrow spine of cliff which was the approach to the cave and a notice which said, 'No passage beyond this point. Dangerous.'

We learned later than only the day before a tourist had fallen into the ravine below the cliff while making the crossing and been badly injured. Our guide had known nothing of this and, aware of the disappointment all seven of us felt, he offered, if we were prepared to follow him in a circumvention of the barbed wire, to take us into the cave nevertheless.

Five of us elected to do so, the other two counting it too foolhardy an enterprise, and proceeded to follow Ibrahim very cautiously. He led us round the barbed wire fence which extended a fairly long way down the rather steep slope - down one side and up the other - placing our hands very carefully between the barbs of the wire for the support without which we would have found it impossible to make either the descent or the ascent required.

We found that this operation was considerably more precarious than we had anticipated but nothing like so precarious as the next stage which involved walking along one narrow ridge which led on to another narrow ridge running transversely to it, which in turn led to a hole in the roof of Cave 4 through which we dropped into the thick layer of dust which covered its floor.

What a tremendous feeling it was to be standing there, ankle-deep in the dust of centuries and looking out of the cave mouth across the shimmering expanse of the Dead Sea. We felt that we were standing in the very dust of history, standing where the now world famous scrolls had lain for so long undetected, standing where no human foot had stood during all these centuries. Personally, these many years afterwards, I still feel something of the thrill I felt then, heightened by the fact that so far as I know no ordinary member of the public has stood there since. At any rate, the embargo against visiting the cave has never been rescinded and the barrier fence has never been removed.

It may be thought that our action, even if prompted by our guide, was stupid and foolhardy; and no doubt it was. It may be said, however, that so far as I was concerned the foolhardiness of the venture was not properly appreciated at the time. It was only when I returned (as a group leader) two years later and viewed Cave 4 from the escarpment facing it on the seaward side that it came home to me. Then, as I walked beyond the Essene monastery ruins situated on that escarpment and arrived at a point immediately opposite the opening to Cave 4 which let me see clearly how deep was the gully below and how narrow the path between the fence and the cave, I caught my breath and felt my knees begin to tremble ever so slightly.

Masada is another place on the Dead Sea that takes us back in dramatic fashion to the first century of the Christian era. Jerome Murphy-O'Connor vividly describes Masada in these terms: 'A great rock curiously like an aircraft-carrier moored to the Western cliffs of the Dead Sea' (*The Holy Land*, p 244); and it is an historical as well as a spectacular site. Standing some two miles inland from the Dead Sea and well over a thousand feet high, this great rock is nowadays a focus of Israeli patriotism because of an event that took place there in 73 AD.

The name Masada means 'stronghold' and it was fortified in about 100

The Lowest Spot on the Earth's Surface

BC. It was, however, Herod the Great in the latter part of the pre-Christian era who made it into the near-impregnable fortress that has come to occupy such an exalted position in Jewish esteem.

After Jerusalem fell to the Romans in 70 AD, a number of fervently nationalistic Jews took refuge in Masada determined to resist to the last drop of their blood. It was three years later before the Roman army finally bested them and the end came in extremely dramatic fashion.

In the latter part of the year 72 AD the Roman Governor, Flavius Silva, decided that enough was enough and that this obdurate rebel group at Masada must be reduced at all costs. Accordingly he invested the fortress and set up a ring of eight siege camps which encircled the entire circumference of Masada - the outline of the camps and of the circumvallation is still startlingly clear when viewed from above. The beleaguered Zealots held out determinedly for a very long time but eventually the Romans succeeded, at enormous cost in terms of the lives of the Jewish prisoners of war whom they had brought with them for just such tasks, in throwing up a ramp on the landward side of the mountain which enabled them to breach the defences.

The breach was finally achieved late in the afternoon of 1st May when the light was beginning to fade. It was clear to all, besiegers and besieged alike, that the issue was now settled and that nothing could prevent the Roman soldiers from sweeping into the fortress as soon as the new day dawned. That evening, the commander of the Jewish garrison, Eleazar Ben Yair, gathered all of the inhabitants of Masada together - there were nearly 1000 men, women and children - and made a speech which has become enshrined for ever in Jewish history.

'We cannot hope to hold out any longer', he told them, 'Tomorrow the Romans will possess Masada. But I have a plan to thwart them of their victory.' His plan was one of mass suicide so that they would avoid slavery and abuse at the hands of their enemy. The plan was approved and carried out so that when the Romans rushed through the broken defences in the morning, they found heap upon heap of corpses, 960 in all, who had chosen death rather than captivity. The only survivors where two women and five children who had somehow hidden themselves in a cave while the suicide pact was being carried out. It was 2nd May 73 AD.

The 'rediscovery', excavation and partial restoration of Masada is a phenomenon of very recent vintage - all of it, in fact, having taken place since 1963. When it was first opened up to tourists in the 1960s, Masada could be reached only on foot. This meant a steep climb up the 'Snake Path' on the seaward side, so-called because of its snake-like ascent of the mountain; or a somewhat shorter, but still quite strenuous, climb on the

93

Travels in the Holy Land

landward side by means of the remains of Silva's ramp.

Today most people make the ascent by means of the cable car which is now in operation. Some, however, choose to use the Snake Path; and some are compelled to use it, like the new soldiers, about to be 'sworn in', whom we sometimes see laboriously climbing up clad in full battle gear and carrying all their battle equipment.

The substantial excavated remains on the top of the mountain reveal what a staggering feat Herod the Great achieved in the building of the immense fortress that was Masada (at what cost, one cannot help wondering, of human life?). Herod, it is true, did not create Masada from scratch. It was first fortified by Alexander Jannaeus half a century or so earlier, but it was Herod who developed it in almost incredible fashion, utilising the whole area of the mountain top - some half a mile long by an eighth of a mile wide - to produce what was to all intents and purposes a garrison town.

He erected a wall round the whole perimeter of the plateau and inside the wall he put everything needed to enable a township to exist - things like cultivated areas, huge water cisterns and food storage caverns. Herod also contrived to make use of the natural contours of the northern end of the mountain to construct for himself a quite luxurious three-tiered palace.

Even today, 2000 years later, the remains to be seen on Masada are irrefutable testimony to the phenomenal feat of construction that Herod brought about in such an unlikely, extremely isolated and difficult spot.

Visiting Masada is a remarkable and never to be forgotten experience. Equally memorable, although totally different, is the experience of swimming in the Dead Sea close by. 'Swimming' is, in fact, a very loose description of what one actually experiences in the waters of the Dead Sea. 'Floating' would be a much more accurate term. The Dead Sea's waters are so buoyant that it is virtually impossible to swim in any normal understanding of the word, just as it is impossible sink. All other oceans consist of water with a salt content of arount 6% but in the Dead Sea the salt content is in the region of 26%. This means that once you get the hang of it, you can, if you wish, sit comfortably in six feet of water and read a book or a newspaper almost as if you were sitting in an armchair.

People often have photographs taken in just such a pose, and some of these can be remarkable in themselves. One year, when a certain book had gained a good deal of notorious publicity, a well-known English bishop had got himself into the aforesaid 'armchair' position in the Dead Sea when one of his group thrust a book into his hands and said, 'Let me take a snap of you, sir, for the diocesan magazine, sitting in the Dead Sea reading a book'. The dear cleric obligingly complied, being unable, lacking his spectacles, to see that the book he was pretending to read from was *Lady Chatterley's Lover*. I often wonder if that picture ever did appear in the diocesan magazine.

The Lowest Spot on the Earth's Surface

The Dead Sea gets its name from the effect produced by its exceptionally high mineral content. For no fish can live in its waters because of that and the reason for the life-denying mineral level is by way of being a sermon in itself.

The basic reason is that the Dead Sea has no outlet. It takes in all the water it can get, from the River Jordan mainly, but it gives none of it away. All the water it loses is lost by evaporation which in the very hot temperatures usually prevailing goes on at a rapid rate, leaving, of course, the minerals behind. It could be said that it is the selfishness of the Dead Sea in refusing to give away any of the water it receives that has condemned it to death.

As it happens, the level of the Dead Sea has dropped to a spectacular extent in the quarter of a century that I have known it. When I first visited it, we used to have our swim (or float) at its northern extremity. We used the changing accommodation at the Hotel Lido closely adjacent to the water's edge. Year by year, however, as the result of the low winter rainfalls accompanied by the pumping of water south from the Sea of Galilee we found the water receding further and further away. Each year we had to walk longer and longer distances from the hotel to the sea. Eventually the hotel had to close and for a long time now it has stood in desolate isolation, empty and abandoned, fully six hundred yards from the water's edge.

Nowadays we generally do our Dead Sea swimming at Ein Gedi. But memories remain of what were fun-filled visits to the Lido in the earlier years. Not least do I remember my first visit. Tim Manson, our so marvellous group leader, realised, no doubt because he was a fellow Presbyterian minister, that my wife and I were not too flush with money and thought he would save us a little here. There was a charge per changing cubicle and Tim, bless him, said to the Arab attendant, 'These are husband and wife. They need only one cubicle between them. Is that all right?' 'Yes, of course', was the reply and he ushered us through the turnstile once I had paid him the amount he asked for. It was only when we reached the cubicles that we discovered that their size made it physically impossible for two adults to change in them at the same time; so I finished up doing a kind of moon dance on the open shore. And, to crown it all, we further discovered that the money the attendant had extracted from me was the price of two admissions.

At the present time there is a considerable commercial exploitation of the mineral resources of the Dead Sea. Some of this can be seen at the north end, where the salt pans glistening in the morning sunlight announce to us tourists travelling down from Jerusalem that we have arrived at the lowest spot on the surface of the earth. But it is at the south end that the first-time visitor is likely to be most astonished at the number and the size of the reclamation factories hard at work extracting the valuable chlorides from the sea. He will not only be astonished but also no doubt somewhat dazzled and thrilled as he sees the salt deposits sparkling all around in their variegated shapes, appearing to the imagination perhaps like some incandescent lunar landscape or like icefloes in a polar sea.

A few miles south of Masada, close to the tip of the Dead Sea, is where Sodom of Biblical notoriety is believed to have stood. Some people say there is a standing pillar of salt in the neighbourhood which is the residue of Lot's wife who, as the Book of Genesis records, was fleeing from the destruction coming upon Sodom and Gomorrah when, contrary to orders, she looked back and was turned into a pillar of salt. I must confess that in all my visits to the Dead Sea I have never yet seen Lot's salty wife but I have seen innumerable bodies plastered thickly all over with black mud.

Between Masada and the factories at the southern extremity an increasing number of hotels have sprung up in recent years. Built very near to the shoreline, they are chiefly to facilitate bathing in the Dead Sea. Israelis flock to these hotels in large numbers in order to take advantage of the therapeutic qualities of the water and of the black mud which covers the seabed at most locations. They spend considerable periods immersed in the sea. They also spread the black Dead Sea mud all over their bodies and let it dry on. This is believed to have beneficial effects on skin ailments such as psoriasis and on joint conditions such as rheumatism and arthritis.

Some distance north of Masada, also close to the shore, lies the oasis of Ein Gedi, which creates a striking area of green in the middle of the brown desolation which characterises most of the Dead Sea coastline. A Jewish settlement was created here in 1947 when the border between Israel and Jordan lay only two miles to the north (as it remained until 1967) and the kibbutz provides bathing and restaurant facilities for visitors. My groups normally utilise them when we make our visit to the Dead Sea.

Ein Gedi means 'spring of the goat' and is mentioned several times in the Old Testament. The best-known of these references is undoubtedly that of 1 Samuel 24 which relates how, in somewhat embarrassingly amusing circmstances, David had Saul, now his enemy, at his mercy but elected to let him go free.

The fact that David found shelter here when pursued by King Saul after the King had turned against him is commemorated by the name given to the spring which creates the oasis. It is called Ein David which means 'David's Fountain'. Ein Gedi owes its quite remarkable abundance of vegetation to this spring, which begins its descent down the mountainside by cascading over the rocks in a very attractive waterfall which is well worth seeing if there is time to climb the path to it.

Nearly every-time the Dead Sea is visited from Jerusalem there is a double reminder of the Good Samaritan parable, because we pass the Inn of the

The Lowest Spot on the Earth's Surface

Good Samaritan both on the outward and on the homeward journey. I always stop there in one direction or the other. What stands there today is a cafe cum shop (although it bears the title 'The Inn of the Good Samaritan') and there never has been an inn there in my acquaintance with the spot.

When I first saw it, the building that occupied the site was an Arab police post with several beautiful Arab horses in the courtyard behind the building. The police post and the horses were casualties of the Six Days' War and for years the place lay more or less deserted until recently it was converted to its present use.

But for centuries this had been traditionally the site of the inn featured in Jesus' famous parable about a Samaritan who befriended a Jewish traveller who had been assaulted and robbed on that brigand-infested highway. There is little doubt that in Jesus' day there actually was an inn located in this vicinity on the Jerusalem-Jericho road and most probably there was also an inn of some kind there for centuries afterwards.

It is true that there is no real evidence that the inn of Jesus' parable stood on this exact spot or even that it was very close to it. But, when I gather my group there and we read the parable, that matters very little. It is enough that we are on the Jerusalem to Jericho road and recalling there the story Jesus centred on it. Its eternal message of 'reach out a helping hand wherever and whenever you can' is thereby imprinted indelibly on our hearts.

Abu Ghosh and Ein Karem

One of the most vivid and also most moving stories in the whole of the New Testament is that told by St Luke of the couple walking home to the village of Emmaus on the first Easter Day who were joined on the way by the Risen Jesus and, after failing at first to recognise him, eventually did so round the supper table in their own home. The strange thing is that today there is great uncertainty as to the location of this Emmaus. No one can say with any certainty 'this is it' or 'it was here.'

Several possibilities are mooted. The one which I personally like best is the present day Abu Ghosh, an Arab village about seven miles from Jerusalem, which is the distance indicated by St Luke's narrative. This was the site also favoured by the Crusaders, who built a magnificent church there, over a spring in the heart of the village. It may well be, of course, that the Crusaders opted for Abu Ghosh as Emmaus because it was convenient and because they liked it for itself.

For my part, since we have as yet no means of knowing the authentic site of Emmaus for sure, I am perfectly content also to opt for Abu Ghosh and for similar reasons. So far as the Christian pilgrim is concerned, whether or not a 'holy place' has a firm authenticity, its main value always is as a kind of visual aid; and to my mind Abu Ghosh provides an excellent visual aid for the Emmaus story and the Resurrection message.

The Crusader church still stands today and is in a very well-preserved condition. In the care of a Benedictine community from Normandy, it continues to be a place of worship. When we sing our psalm and read the Emmaus narrative beside the spring which flows through the crypt, the events of that Emmaus walk of long ago come very close and we find ourselves re-echoing with personal conviction the words of the disciples, 'It is true: the Lord has risen'.

Abu Ghosh and Ein Karem

The name Abu Ghosh was, in fact, the name of a brigand chief who occupied the village in the early nineteenth century, made it his headquarters and exacted a toll from travellers passing through. The land was at this time under Turkish rule but the authorities decided that it was in their better interest to permit him to stay there rather than face the trouble of attempting to drive him out. And they even allowed him to rename the village after himself.

Previously it was known as Kiryat Yearim under which name we meet it often in the Old Testament. In particular, it was the village where the Ark of the Covenant found a resting place for the twenty year period between its being given back by the Philistines and its being transported to Jerusalem by King David. When you ascend the massive stone steps that lead from the crypt below into the church above, you find that this event is commemorated by an illuminated replica of the Ark of the Covenant which is to be seen in a recess beside the altar.

One of the things that endeared Abu Ghosh so much to the Crusaders was that it was from the hill overlooking the church on the seaward side that many of them caught their first sight of the Holy City as they marched in from the coast. On that height, which is in fact where the original village was located, there now stands high the Church of Our Lady of the Ark of the Covenant. It is distinguished by its massive statue of Mary with the baby Jesus in her arms standing on top of the church and looking across to Jerusalem on the distant skyline.

Not for any reason of ecclesiastical or historical congruity but simply as a matter of practical convenience, it is normal practice to take the group to Ein Karem on the same day as it visits Abu Ghosh. The journey between Abu Ghosh and Ein Karem is a delight in itself. Few would contend that the countryside in the immediate vicinity of Jerusalem merits being described as pretty. It is in the main rugged and even harsh but much of it nevertheless carries its own undeniable attractiveness. The country roads by which our bus conveys us from Abu Ghosh to Ein Karem are very attractive and at times quite spectacular. This is especially so when, shortly after departing from Abu Ghosh, we leave the highway and drive some distance up into the mountains. This presents us with a stupendous view down into the valley far beneath us and across to the imposing structure of the Hadassah Hospital high up on the other side, before we embark on a strikingly picturesque descent to the valley floor.

Hadassah Hospital, well-known and much respected in its own right, is world-famous for the Chagall windows which adorn the synagogue situated beside its main entrance. These are twelve stained glass creations of the renowned sculptor Chagall representing the twelve tribes of Israel.

Travels in the Holy Land

Once in the valley it is only a short journey to the village of Ein Karem (literally, 'Spring of the Vineyard'). Known to the Crusaders as St John in the Mountains, Ein Karem has been identified from early times as the birthplace of John the Baptist; and two churches at opposite ends of the village pay homage to that fact today.

On one side of the valley in which the village stands is the Church of the Visitation which commemorates the visit of Mary to her cousin Elizabeth when both were pregnant. In the crypt is to be seen a spring which, according to a tradition of the middle ages, sprung out of the hillside when Mary and Elizabeth met at this very point. The crypt also contains a little cave-like opening in a side wall in which, so a legend runs, Elizabeth hid her child, John, to protect him from the murdering hands of the soldiers of Herod when they were in the area killing all the children under two years of age in Herod's infamous 'Massacre of the Innocents'.

On the other side of the valley is the Church of St John and this is believed to stand over the place where John the Baptist was born. Apart from its claim on our interest because of this, the church of St John commands special attention from many of its visitors on account of the remarkable collection of paintings that adorns its walls, especially an El Greco.

My own most remarkable memory of Ein Karem concerns one of my group members, Mary Duda. It was not until we were actually in the bus and on our way to Ein Karem that she confided in me that this particular visit was very, very special to her and why. Born in Poland, she had been evacuated along with others from Poland to Ein Karem for safety's sake when war erupted in 1939 and had spent six years of her childhood there until the war ended in 1945. It was now 1988 and it was the first time she had been back to Ein Karem since her evacuation period was concluded.

It was, of course, a highly emotional experience for her to be returning to Ein Karem with all its connotations for her and after so long a time. Once we learned of the circumstances all the rest of us shared in that emotion to a considerable extent.

Mary vividly remembered attending Mass regularly in the Church of St John and when we actually entered the church she found her recollections enhanced and sharpened. When we re-emerged from the church and were standing at the top of the flight of steps leading up to its front door, Mary was able to pinpoint from that vantage point and with ill-suppressed excitement a number of places in the village that she recognised, including the school and the house where she had been fostered during these evacuation years. A conversation with the priest, despite the limitations necessarily imposed by his being Spanish and having come to Ein Karem only recently, was also deeply moving for her as she spoke with him of the village and its people.

But the best was yet to come. As Mary and I took leave of the priest and came down the church steps to follow after the rest of the group who had already moved on to where the bus was waiting, an old lady walked into the church compound accompanied by a dog. Just as we passed her, the old lady called out something - unintelligible to me - to the dog which had run on ahead.

'That was Polish', Mary said to me in a fever of excitement, 'She was speaking in Polish'.

'You must speak to her, then', I said, 'She may be able to tell you much more than the priest could with his limited English and his only recent acquaintance with the village.'

So I called to the old lady, took Mary across to her and left them chattering to each other in Polish while I went to inform the others that our departure from Ein Karem would need to be postponed a few minutes more, and why.

Some time later Mary rejoined us in a seventh heaven of astonished delight. The old lady, who was herself Polish, remembered the evacuees coming to the village during the war and had been able to bring Mary up to date about many Ein Karem things and many Ein Karem people.

I was surprised that Mary had kept her previous Ein Karem connection to herself until we were on the very point of visiting it and I offered to arrange for her to be brought back by taxi to spend a whole day or part of a day there wandering around and renewing old memories. She expressed her gratitude for the suggestion but declined it.

She felt that she was not yet ready for that. To have bridged a gap of forty-three years as she had done that day was as much emotional impact as she reckoned she was able to cope with meantime. But it had been absolutely wonderful, she said, and now that the bridge between the past and the present had been made, she fully intended to cross over it again soon. I am sure that she will.

Around the New City of Jerusalem

There are really two Jerusalems in the present day. There is the old walled city which has a predominantly Arab population with an increasing admixture of Jews; and there is the New City which is almost exclusively Jewish. The total population is in the region of half a million of whom around 150,000 live in the Old City. Since the bulk of the Christian holy places of Jerusalem are in or adjacent to the Old City, it is that which commands most of the attention and the time of the Christian pilgrim. But the majority of pilgrims take or make time to see also something of what the New City has to offer. Sometimes a New City Tour is built into the scheduled itinerary, sometimes it is offered as an 'optional extra', sometimes individual members of a party, either singly or in small groups, 'do their own thing' in this regard. One way or another, few pilgrims miss out altogether on the New City.

A typical half day visit to the New City is likely to include the Shrine of the Book in the Hebrew Museum, the Model of second century Jerusalem and the Yad Vashem, as well as a tour round the Knesset, the Parliament Offices, the University Campus and the main streets of the city. Let me tell you first of all a little about the drive round the city.

The Knesset is the building in which the Parliament of Israel convenes. In close proximity to it are the various government offices and, this being the Government Centre, the whole is given the name Hakirya which literally means 'the City'. Opposite the entrance to the Knesset is sited a massive Menora, the menora being the seven-branched candelabrum which is the symbol of Israel. The huge Menora across from the Knesset, which we usually make a point of viewing close up, was the gift of the British Parliament to the newly formed State of Israel, as a token of friendship and goodwill.

Around the New City of Jerusalem

Standing about 16 feet high and 13 feet wide and cast in bronze, it presents a very imposing appearance. Its seven branches contain no less than twenty-nine decorated panels which represent in relief important people and important events in Jewish history. There are not many visitors to Jerusalem who have not had their photograph taken in front of this Menora; and we discovered on one visit that it was not only tourists who had this desire. As we were standing in front of the Menora, engaged in our various activities - studying the relief panels, looking across to the Knesset, photographing or being photographed - a car whirled up beside us and disgorged a newly married bride and bridegroom, resplendent in all their wedding finery. They were there to have *their* photographs taken in front of the Menora on this special day; and we learned that this was a practice regularly followed by Jerusalem wedding couples.

The Campus of the Hebrew University stretches southwards from the Government offices area and occupies a most pleasant site. Tourists, however, may well be confused nowadays when they hear mention of the University Campus because the reference could be to any one of three different entities. Prior to the ending of the British Mandate in 1947 and the ensuing conflict that issued in the partition settlement of 1948, the Hebrew University was situated on Mount Scopus, across the valley from Jerusalem. When the partition placed Mount Scopus outside of Israel, the new State of Israel proceeded to build a replacement Hebrew University within its own territory and constructed a magnificent campus close to the Knesset. Since Mount Scopus came under Israeli control following the 1967 war, a new University campus has come into being there which is still expanding.

Very near to the Knesset and to the University is the Israeli Museum. Because of the demands of their itinerary, touring groups like ours are usually able to devote time to visit in the Museum complex no more than the Shrine of the Book. Nevertheless there is a great deal more to see and enjoy when time is available, particularly in the realms of art and archaeology. The Shrine of the Book is, however, the chief focus of interest for most visitors.

Designed in its outward appearance to look like an enlarged version of one of the jars in which the Dead Sea Scrolls were secreted until the excitement of their discovery in 1948, the Shrine of the Book is an underground repository for the scrolls and a stupendous example of what modern skill and technology can accomplish. Here these priceless scrolls are on display in a temperature-controlled atmosphere that safeguards them against deterioration; and it is unlikely that anyone could walk round the display without catching his or her breath not only at the remarkable scrolls themselves but also at their place of safe custody.

At the same time, although I am in no doubt that the scrolls, immensely valuable as they are, are in a much better and more secure state of preservation in their present habitat, I cannot completely obliterate a little nostalgia for the imaginativeness and romanticism of the setting in which I first saw them. That was in 1965 when they were housed in the Rockefeller Museum in East Jerusalem, then part of Jordan. They were presented there in a series of make-believe caves whose tableaux helped to conjure up in one's mind a vivid picture of the story of the scrolls being hidden away for safe keeping in caves beside the Dead Sea, lying there undetected and unsuspected for nineteen centuries and then by the merest accident being brought out into the glare of world publicity.

Following the Israeli military conquest of 1967, the Dead Sea Scrolls were removed from the Rockefeller Museum and the marvel of their present home was built to accommodate them.

In the same neighbourhood as the Knesset, the University and the Museum, we are able to catch a clear sight from the bus, as we drive along the main road, of a large and imposing ecclesiastical structure, standing in the valley below the highway. This is the Monastery of the Cross. It catches the eye not only because of its size and structure but also because it is a very old building surrounded on all sides by modern ones. A church once stood here in Byzantine times and the monastery was erected on the site in the eleventh century. Its name is derived from a tradition that the wood which formed the cross on which Jesus was crucified came from a tree that grew on this very spot. Originally Georgian (founded by King Bagrat of Georgia) the Monastery of the Cross was sold in 1685 to the Greek Orthodox Church in whose possession it remains.

Another place in the New City that is well worth a visit from any tourist is the Holy Land Hotel - not for a drink or a meal but for the magnificent Model of the Jerusalem of 66 AD that is on view in its grounds. The Model occupies an area of several hundred square yards and, constructed on a scale of 1 to 50, it gives an astonishingly detailed representation of the city of Jerusalem as it was in the first century of the Christian era - or, at least, how some authorities reckoned that it looked. A great deal of careful research went into the project but, not surprisingly, a number of the final decisions made about the topography of the city of the time had to contain a certain element of speculation. Nevertheless, the resulting production gives a very vivid and, on the whole, probably a reasonably accurate portrayal of Herodian Jerusalem. The actual construction is a marvel in itself, crafted skillfully and painstakingly in stone.

Having spent some time wandering round the Model and listening perhaps to the taped explanations which are available in different languages at the press of a button at various vantage points, we may well travel on next

Around the New City of Jerusalem

to the Yad Vashem, the extremely moving, sometimes harrowing, Holocaust Museum. Erected on Mount Memorial, the adjoining height to Mount Hertzl, the Yad Vashem was created in 1957 in memory of the 6 million Jews who were massacred by the Nazis in the course of the Second World War. The name Yad Vashem means 'Monument and Memorial' and is derived from a reference in Isaiah 56.5.

The main memorial building contains a host of archive material of various kinds, including a vast amount of film, along with a record of all who were killed. Many people, however, find the most deeply moving part of the whole memorial complex to be the Hall of Remembrance, which consists simply of a large open hall made of unhewn boulders with a mosaic floor bearing an eternal flame and twenty-one names of the largest concentration and death camps such as Belsen, Dachau and Auschwitz.

Two other prominent New City buildings of a much different kind from any so far mentioned but also wellknown far beyond the borders of Israel are the YMCA and the King David Hotel.

The YMCA may well be the most impressive YMCA structure anywhere in the world. It was built in 1928 through the generosity of an American millionaire who donated a million dollars to the project and what resulted is one of the most prestigious buildings in the whole of Jerusalem. Apart from its highly esteemed accommodation facilities, the Jerusalem 'Y' has two particularly outstanding features. One is its high tower, from which an unmatched panoramic view of the city may be seen. The other is the mosaic reproduction, on the entrance floor, of the famous sixth century Madaba map of Jerusalem. This map was part of a larger map of the Holy Land and was discovered on the floor of a Byzantine church at Madaba, east of the Jordan River.

Another considerably less significant feature of the Jerusalem YMCA to whose attractiveness I can personally testify is the quality of their chips (or french fries, if you so prefer). One evening after dinner, during a stay in the Scottish Hospice at St Andrew's, we strolled as a group into the New City, especially to have a look at the King David Hotel and the YMCA. Eventually we found our way into the YMCA restaurant in order to sample their tea and cream cakes which had been warmly recommended to us. When it came to the point, although the rest adhered to the original intention and ordered cream cakes of varying kinds, I succumbed to an inner craving and asked if I might have a plate of chips. This request occasioned much hilarity among the rest of the group and produced many expressions of mock horror at the way in which my plebeian tastes were causing them embarrassment. The strange thing was that when my chips were served, every single member of the group contrived to beg or steal a chip (or two) from my plate - a rather noble act of condescension, I thought, forcing themselves down to my lowly level in that way.

The King David Hotel is still one of the best in Jerusalem but, sadly, it is probably best known and best remembered for the bomb that exploded in it during the stormy times that preceded the ending of the British Mandate. Part of the hotel was demolished and scores of British servicemen and others were killed and many more maimed. Most people remember something of the horror of that carnage but the day it came home to me with greatest impact was when I was walking past the King David in the company of David Abassi, a tour guide.

'I was a sergeant in the Palestine Police during the Mandate', he said, 'and our police post was just a few yards along the road there from the hotel. On the day of the explosion, I was sent to the King David Hotel with a message for the British commanding officer stationed in it. I had just left the hotel and was walking back to my post when the bomb went off. If I had been a minute later in delivering my message I would not have been walking here with you today.'

Hebron: David's First Capital

To take the road south from Bethlehem is to find oneself entering a luscious and fertile land. As we draw nearer and nearer to Hebron, we come upon an increasingly luxuriant display of grapes and other fruits in the fields all around; and when we have travelled ten miles from Bethlehem we enter Hebron itself.

Hebron's history stretches far back into antiquity and one of its numerous claims to fame is that for seven and a half years it was David's capital, his first. It remained his capital until he conquered Jerusalem and adopted it as his capital instead. But Hebron's entry upon the historical scene goes much further back even than David. It goes back to the time when Abraham bought the Cave of Machpelah from Ephron the Hittite for use as a burial place for his wife Sarah.

In the course of time it became a family burial vault, as in addition to Sarah, Abraham himself and also Isaac and Rebecca, Leah and Jacob were laid to rest in it - in Jacob's case after his body had been brought back from Egypt. Today, as has been the case for centuries, the Cave of Machpelah is in many respects the centrepiece of Hebron. Surrounded by a huge wall which now encloses a large mosque built over the burial place, the cave is visibly at the centre of the town geographically. More than that, however, it continues to dominate the history of Hebron as it has done for hundreds of years.

The significant fact is, of course, that it is the Tomb of the Patriarchs. Herod the Great built his massive wall in order to enclose the place of burial and that wall superbly built as it was, though so long ago, is very well preserved, and probably the best preserved of all the many Herodian structures still surviving. 'Massive' is perhaps the only word adequate to describe it, some of its blocks being no less than 36 by 9 feet. Its massiveness has given rise to an Arab legend that it was really built by Solomon assisted by demons.

Travels in the Holy Land

Sacred to three religions, Jewish, Christian and Moslem, the Cave of Machpelah was surmounted by a Christian church in Byzantine times and the Crusaders built a church there, too, when they were in the Holy Land. Later the Crusader church was converted into a large Moslem mosque. With the Six Days' War of 1967 and the coming of Israeli rule, most of the mosque was turned into a museum, with a synagogue being installed within it and a small part reserved near the entrance, suitably carpeted, for the continuing use of Moslems. The Moslems come here for prayer four times a day and have it all to themselves on their holy day (Friday) when Jews are not permitted to enter. The mosque contains a splendid Mihrab (the *niche* to which Moslems turn in prayer) and on its right there is an exquisitely constructed wooden pulpit (or Minbar) which was made in 1091 for a mosque in Ashkelon and gifted in 1191 by Saladin to the mosque in Hebron.

It is not possible nowadays to enter the Cave of Machpelah itself. The nearest we can get is to peer down through a small aperture to see a small lamp glowing in the darkness below. As a matter of fact, it is thought that no one at all has set foot in the Cave since the Crusaders did so in the twelfth century. In 1119 they penetrated into it and, finding there a collection of human bones, they bathed the bones in wine before securely sealing up the burial place once again - and so far as is known, no one has been inside it since.

There are, of course, other points of interest in Hebron. Two of these are their glass blowing and their pottery making. Like the town itself, the story of these industries in Hebron goes back into the very mists of time. In the period when David was exercising his kingship in Hebron, glass was being blown and pottery was being crafted in the selfsame place. These industries continue to flourish in Hebron and it is quite fascinating to go and watch the craftsmen at work, which they are very willing to have tourists do.

There are a number of small glass-blowing factories at the side of the main road and it is the easiest thing in the world for the bus to draw in and let us disembark for a time to spectate at the glassblowing operation and perhaps to buy some samples of the finished product. The intense heat and dazzle from the open furnaces seem to accord strangely with the apparent casualness of the men as they thrust their long rods into the fire; and yet with a few puffs here, a few twists there and a sharp tap or two, in what seems no time at all vases and bowls, glasses and medallions are produced in different designs and colours.

To look on at the potter fashioning the soft clay on his wheel causes many of us to think of Jeremiah, commanded by the Lord to do just what we are doing. Of course, the potter of Jeremiah's day did not have the assistance of electrical power to rotate his wheel but, apart from that, it is the same skill, handed down through many centuries, that we see demonstrated and in much the same fashion. How rapidly the wheel revolves and how fast the potter's hands move as he shapes and moulds the clay; and how strikingly symmetrical the finished product. Having watched the expert at work, it is a bit daunting, if thrilling, when the potter vacates his seat at the wheel and invites some of us to 'have a go'. The leader (fortunately) is usually able to adopt the very unselfish attitude that he must not seize this opportunity for himself but must rather insist that the rest of the group have prior claim on it. The result is that the leader avoids being the one who under the intense scrutiny of his or her peers turns out a misshapen, lopsided pot that would be fit only for the rubbish heap were it not for the fact that, as in Jeremiah's day, the clay vessel - like human lives in God's hands - can be reshaped into something worthwhile by the master craftsman.

The giant mosque in the heart of Hebron has always had a mingling of Jewish and Moslem elements; inevitably so on account of the fact that the Patriarchs buried beneath it are sacred to both religions. Hence the alternation, and now the duality, of use of the building enclosed by the vast Herodian walls. This mingling of the Jewish and the Moslem is illustrated in a quaint sort of way by the juxtaposition of two ancient traditions, one Jewish and one Arab. The old Jewish tradition is to the effect that the Cave of Machpelah is also the burial place of Adam and Eve who came to live in Hebron after they were expelled from the Garden of Eden. Linked closely with this tradition is the circumstance that Hebron is also known by the Jewish name Kiryath-Arba which means 'The Town of the Four', the 'four' being the four couples buried there - Abraham and Sarah, Isaac and Rachel, Jacob and Leah, Adam and Eve. The Arab tradition centres upon one of the stones in a corner of the floor of the mosque. This particular stone has a pronounced depression in it which, the tradition says, was made by Adam's left foot as a result of his standing so often on that very spot to say his prayers.

Whatever may be said about these traditions, one inescapable fact about the Jewish-Moslem dimension of the Tomb of the Patriarchs is that it has been a source of potential discord ever since the Israelis took the town under their control in 1967. Time after time since then that potential has erupted into violence and since the *intifada* it has not been considered prudent to take touring groups into Hebron.

Consequently, so long as the *intifada* continues, tourists are unlikely also to be able to visit the famous Oak of Mamre. This very old and very large oak tree is to be found some distance outside the town. Fenced off nowadays, it is reputed to be where Abraham and Sarah received the celestial visitors who informed them that despite their advanced years they were to produce a son and thereafter many descendants. The tree standing there today, and highly revered, is about 600 years old; and it is owned by the Russian Orthodox Church which has built a monastery close beside it.

On the way back from Hebron to Bethlehem we are likely to make a brief stop at the Pools of Solomon. These are three large reservoirs located quite close to the main road and until fairly recently it was widely accepted that Solomon had built them. An old tradition had it that in Ecclesiastes 2:6 we had Solomon referring to this fact: 'I made me pools of water, to water therewith the wood that bringeth forth trees'. It is now recognised that the Pools were in fact built by Pontius Pilate in order to provide a water supply for Jerusalem, transporting the water from the reservoirs by means of a pipeline which skirted Bethlehem and some of whose remains can be seen near Bethlehem still.

The Rose Red City

What might have been in 1965, and what really should have been in 1965, that is, my first visit to Petra, 'the rose red city half as old as time', did not take place until 1967.

It was in the course of my first ever pilgrimage to the Holy Land - under the leadership of Tim Manson - that the opportunity first came to visit Petra. It was a whole day trip, offered as an optional extra and my wife and I ought, of course, to have jumped at the chance. Looking back it seems utterly foolish and almost inexcusable that we did not; and yet, given the choice all over again in the same circumstances, we would almost certainly have passed up the opportunity again.

No doubt a number of factors contributed to our ultimate decision not to go. There was the cost: £8 each (!) was a lot of extra money for us to pay out in those impecunious days. There were the physical demands of the trip: a 4 am departure, four hours' car ride at speed through the desert either way and a very late return to the hotel. There was the obligatory horseback ride through the narrow mile and a half long ravine that is the only entrance to Petra: neither of us had ever ridden a horse before and we knew there had been accidents in previous years through people falling off their horses in the Siq, as the entrance pass was called. There was the horrific disaster that had only recently occurred: a sudden thunderstorm while some tourists were riding through the Siq had caused a flash flood that had engulfed them in the narrow confines of the ravine and several had been drowned.

The chief reason, however, which would probably have been sufficient of itself to deter us from going to Petra that day, was that we had struck up a friendship with two other members of the group who had very special plans for the same day. Olive Patrick and her companion, Mrs Black, had taken good care not to ask if we would accompany them, but we had no doubt that they would feel greatly helped if we went with them on the 'Petra day' to visit the grave of Olive's sister in the neighbourhood of Bethlehem.

She and Olive had been together on a similar Holy Land tour the previous year and had taken the optional tour to Petra. On the horseback ride through the Siq, Helen's horse had been suddenly startled by something or other and had shied and reared. The result was that Helen had been thrown from the saddle. In her fall she struck her head against a stone and suffered an injury so severe that she died without regaining consciousness. Helen had been buried in a cemetery near to Bethlehem and Inter-Church Travel had invited Olive to come with a friend on this tour so that she might have the opportunity of visiting the grave. The plan was to make the visit on the day set aside for the Petra tour; and we decided to go with them.

Tim Manson also forewent the Petra trip in order to accompany Olive and Mrs Black on their mission. It was a mission that proved much more difficult to accomplish than any of us had anticipated, for it turned out a far from easy task to locate the cemetery in which Helen had been interred. Olive, understandably, had only the vaguest idea of its location, except that it was in the Bethlehem area, and at first no one we asked in or around the town seemed to have any knowledge of it. In the end, however, after a number of false scents had been followed and with the assistance of our very patient taxi-driver, we found what we were looking for.

It was a pretty rough and ill-tended burial place, to be sure, but the grave we sought was there and a seemly headstone had been erected. We paid our respects to Helen, we shared in a moving little service that Tim conducted; and Olive was so pleased and grateful to have us there with her that we no longer had any lingering doubts about whether or not we had been right to turn our backs on the Petra opportunity.

This feeling was reinforced later in the day when Tim held a Communion service in the Garden of Gethsemane for those who had not gone to Petra. His little congregation (a few others had chosen not to go to Petra) gathered under and around the oldest of the eight old olive trees that grew in the Garden; and it was an exceedingly moving experience to share in the Communion service in that very special place.

Two years later I did get to Petra, although unfortunately my wife was not with me on this occasion. It was towards the end of May 1967. The drums of approaching war were sounding in the Middle East but I was leading a Holy Land pilgrimage for the very first time and I was deaf to the drums. None of my group heard them either or if they did, they failed to understand the message they were beating out. Some two weeks later came the Six Days' War which resulted in a decisive Israeli victory and the annexation of the Jordanian territory on the West of the Jordan River. This made a visit to Petra from Jerusalem a much more difficult, onerous and time-demanding enterprise and I have so far, to my great regret, not been back. But I did visit Petra in that spring of 1967 and the visit remains an indelible memory.

As it would have been in 1965, going to Petra meant a very early rise in order to pile into the fleet of Mercedes saloon cars lined up at the hotel door ready to transport us to our destination. We had no breakfast before we left - and no great desire for any at four o'clock in the morning when a quickly brewed cup of tea was quite sufficient, thank you - but we had the rather romantic promise of breakfast in the desert en route.

Once all were safely aboard, the fleet of cars raced off at breakneck speed on the 200 miles-plus journey that would eventually bring us to Petra. It was a thrilling journey as we careered into the wilderness and (shortly) into the dawn. Some two hours later, by which time we were about halfway to Petra, we stopped for our promised and now much needed breakfast. The sun was well up but the morning was still fresh and everyone was affected in some measure by the romanticism of it all - making a breakfast stop in the heart of the desert. In itself the breakfast was a very ordinary affair. The roadside cafe where we ate was rather nondescript, the facilities it had to offer were no more than adequate (although necessary), and the food was nothing special. But we were hungry and caught up in a feeling of adventure and we enjoyed the desert breakfast experience immensely. It was therefore with renewed vigour and enthusiasm that we set off on the second leg of our long journey.

After another two hours' hard driving we stopped again, just where the monotony of the desert that had surrounded the road in unbroken fashion for so long was replaced by green land. This, we were told, was the beginning of the Wadi Musa (Valley of Moses) and we would arrive at the entrance to Petra at the valley's other extremity. It was here, tradition has it, that Moses struck the rock with his staff and caused water to gush forth; and, the tradition continues, the stream that irrigates the valley today is the very stream brought into being by that action of Moses.

We stopped only long enough to take photographs and sample the water before continuing on our way. Before we had travelled much further, we were able to see ahead of us a range of mountains standing out improbably but spectacularly against the skyline and bringing to an abrupt end the flat country through which we were presently journeying. This, then, was our first sight of the mysterious city of Petra or, at least, of where Petra was located. As yet we were unable to see anything of the city itself; but we knew that it was enclosed in those mountains and that soon we would pass through the entrance and see it for ourselves.

Our arrival was expected and horses, each with a young lad as attendant, were in readiness for us. It was with no little trepidation that we mounted for, although we were assured the beasts were very docile and obedient, most of the group were like me and had never ridden a horse before. Off we set, then, each of us with his boy, armed with a stick, to look after horse and rider. Before long we plunged into the Siq. This is a very narrow ravine that splits the hundred foot high cliffs, so narrow that for most of its length it would seem possible to stretch out one's arms and touch both sides at once, hence the disastrous effect of the flash flood of 1965.

The Siq is like a long tunnel, winding its narrow path this way and that. Its walls are so close and so high that most of the light is shut out and you lose practically all sight of the sky above. There is, however, enough light, although of a subdued character, for us to see and marvel.

It was obvious that the horses had made this journey many a time and were bored by it, plodding along in totally disinterested fashion as they picked their route carefully among the stones and boulders that littered the track. The boy in charge of my horse was clearly anxious, if he could, to relieve the monotony for himself by stirring the beast into a trot, or even a canter. To my absolute horror he dealt it several sharp blows with his stick and shouted fiercely at it, all the while darting mischievous glances in my direction. If his hope was to give me a scare, he certainly was successful. What I would have done if that horse had got up any speed at all, I shudder to think. Fortunately for me, it was old and tired and unresponsive. To my unbounded relief it was content just to plod along at the same pace.

For the boy and his horse, who had done it so many times, the passage through the Siq may well have been a terrible bore. But for us who had never done it before, it was almost magical; and our first glimpse into Petra itself was nothing short of breathtaking. As we reached almost to the end of the narrow defile that is the Siq, suddenly, framed by the slit that was the end of the ravine, we caught partial sight of a stupendous high building carved directly out of the reddish-brown cliff face opposite. Petra contains many temples and this is the best known of them all. It was long believed to have treasure hidden in the large Roman vase which stands above it and so came to be known as the Treasury of Pharaoh. When we emerged from the Siq, we could see the whole of the Treasury and marvel not only at its size but also at the skill, the ingenuity and the daring that enabled the Nabataeans to create such a beautiful edifice out of the very cliff.

The Nabataeans it was who built Petra. They were an Arab tribe who first settled there eight centuries before Christ; and they probably selected the site quite deliberately for its strategic value. It certainly became for them in later years an ideal headquarters from which they could operate a system of exacting toll from all passing trade, without any fear of reprisal. Not only was it close beside the regular trade routes but its situation, with mountains surrounding it and entrance possible only through one narrow pass, enabled the Nabataeans to build an impregnable fortress from which they could foray at will to demand their protection money and their percentages. The Nabataean period of domination lasted until the end of the first century AD.

The city they created is one of the marvels of the ancient world. Occupying an area about a mile long and varying in width from 500 to 200 yards, and totally encircled by mountains, Petra defies adequate description, least of all from one who has visited it only once, for one afternoon, and that more than twenty years ago. All I would venture to say is that the impact it made on me has remained and my memories of its fascinating loveliness are still astonishingly vivid. Constructed from the local sandstone, predominantly reddish-brown in colour but veined in a remarkable multi-coloured fashion, the houses and other buildings whose remains are all over the open valley floor are accompanied by a host of houses, tombs and temples that have been carved straight out of the rock face of the mountains that enclosed and guarded the city.

On the return journey to Jerusalem, as the cars sped back through the desert, we met a large number of military convoys and saw a lot of troops. At one stage the driver of the car I was in turned on the radio and we heard an excited voice shouting in Arabic. The driver turned to me, who was sitting beside him, and said, with a broad smile, 'Nasser'.

The drums of war were sounding all right, even if we did not understand their message. Two weeks later the Arabs and the Israelis were locked in combat.

A Trip to the Seaside

It is always a pleasant addition to the main touring programme to make an optional tour from Jerusalem to Jaffa, even when the bus happens to develop a flat tyre. The first part of the journey is not new to us as we take the main Tel Aviv road but not long after we pass the cut-off for Abu Ghosh we leave the highway and take a cross-country route to the coast, passing on the way a number of places of Biblical interest.

First of all there is Latrun, one of three suggested sites for the Emmaus of the Easter story. It must be said that this is not in the least the probable true location of the New Testament Emmaus but it was the one that tradition favoured for a very long time. The reason was that some old manuscripts of the Gospels give the distance from Jerusalem to Emmaus as 160 stadia which fits in with the Latrun site almost exactly. But modern scholarship has established to general agreement that the more likely correct reading is 60 stadia which is, in fact, more closely akin to the limit of a 'Sabbath day's journey'. This would rule out Latrun and, incidentally, fit in with Abu Ghosh since its distance from Jerusalem is just that (and I have already indicated my personal preference for Abu Ghosh as the site of Emmaus).

Until 1967 there was an Arab village called Imwas (a version of the name Emmaus) close by where the monastery of Latrun stands and on a site now known as Canada Park. In that year the inhabitants were all evacuated and the village was totally razed to the ground. So came the end of a place that had been home to a human population since at least the second century before Christ. The belief that it was to be identified with the biblical Emmaus was certainly in vogue by the fourth century AD, by which time it was known by its new Roman name of Nicopolis, and may well go further back in time. A Christian church was built here in the Byzantine era and in their time the Crusaders erected another on the same site. Only the ruins of the Crusader church are to be seen today.

116

What *is* to be seen in all its glory less than half a mile away is the Monastery of the Trappist Fathers of Latrun. Its sheer beauty is enhanced by the situation it occupies on an eminence overlooking the surrounding plain and is enhanced even more when you approach close enough to see the colourful gardens that front it.

Leaving Latrun and continuing our cross-country route towards Jaffa, we pass by the village of Eshtaol which is adjacent to the ruins of Zorah, the place where the mighty Samson was born nearly 3000 years ago. This whole area is full of places evocative of Old Testament story, including the Valley of Sorek, the home of Delilah who has gone down in history as both Samson's great love and his ruin; and the Valley of Elah which witnessed David's famous conflict with the giant Philistine champion, Goliath. The Valley of Elah derives its name from the elah (terebinth) tree which grows in profusion in the district. The valley runs all the way to Bethlehem, David's home town. A stream flowing in it has the name David's Brook; and the tradition is that it was from this very stream that the young shepherd boy, David, gathered the five smooth stones to take with him as he went out to do battle with Goliath and one of which he used to kill him. Who knows, the tradition may be true. At any rate, to stop the bus and get out to stand beside the brook, perhaps with some of its pebbles in one's hand, is very likely to project oneself back through many hundreds of years and conjure up a picture of that historic conflict and its astonishing outcome, taking place not far away.

It is, of course, Jaffa that is our chief objective on this tour and we are not likely to be disappointed in it. The Hebrew version of its name is Yafo and there is a tradition that claims it took the name from Japheth, son of Noah, who established the town after the Flood subsided. The history of Jaffa no doubt reaches far back into antiquity but it is much more likely that the name Yafo is an adaptation of the Hebrew word for 'beautiful' which is Yafe.

The town is given its earliest mention in known history when it is listed among the places captured by Thutmose III. in 1468 BC. For nearly three centuries after that it remained in Egyptian hands until the Philistines gained control over it around 1200 BC. In succeeding centuries sovereignty over Jaffa passed from nation to nation - the Israelites, the Philistines once more, the Israelites again, and then Assyria, Egypt, Babylon, Persia, Sidon, Greece, Egypt, Syria in that order, before yet again becoming Jewish in the closing decades of the first century before Christ.

During all these centuries Jaffa owed its importance and its desirability to the fact that it was one of the chief seaports of the land. It was, for instance, to the harbour of Jaffa that King Hiram of Tyre promised to ship cedar wood from Lebanon to assist Solomon in his building of the Temple at Jerusalem. It declined in importance after Herod built a new port at Caesarea but only for a time. After a while the port of Caesarea itself diminished in importance by virtue of the fact that its harbour began to silt up. Consequently, Jaffa came to the forefront again as a major seaport and from that time on it continued to occupy a prominent position as such until the present century, not least during the Crusades.

Jaffa was predominantly Arab when the British Mandate came to an end and became involved in much fierce Arab-Jewish fighting in the conflict that ensued. Since then it has been a mainly Jewish town with a few Arabs and a few Christians. The theory that its name is linked with a word that means 'beautiful' has much to commend it when you actually visit it. To stand on the seafront of Tel Aviv, just a mile or two to the north, and look across the bay to see Jaffa thrusting out into the sparkling blue waters of the Mediterranean is to recognise how fitting is that explanation.

The Greeks in their time called it Joppa and it is under that name we encounter it in the New Testament. It was while the Apostle Peter was staying in the house of Simon the Tanner in Joppa that he received the heavenly vision that instructed him that non-Jews also should be welcomed into the Christian church (Acts 10). It was in Joppa that Peter met the devout Christian believer, Tabitha (Dorcas in Greek), who 'spent all her time doing good and helping the poor' (Acts 9).

Our visit to present-day Jaffa is always a pleasant experience. Not only because of the interest inherent in strolling round an old, historic, town which has so much to display of its past. Not only because of the striking outlook across the bay in the direction of Tel Aviv. Not only because of the fascinating incongruity of the new Artists' Quarter situated on the hill above the harbour and just beside the Franciscan Monastery of St Peter. Not only because of the colourful attractiveness of the harbour itself. For us, usually Christian, and often Scottish, tourists, there are two other things we particularly want to do.

One is to visit the House of Simon the Tanner but this, it must be admitted, often does not match up to expectations, because we do not always manage to gain admission. This is not because we have somehow or other managed to debar ourselves by committing some misdemeanour. No, it is a simple matter of not always succeeding in eliciting an answer to our ringing of the doorbell. Despite presenting ourselves between the proper hours as indicated on the notice on the door and ringing the bell as the notice instructs us to do if we wish admission, there is, I have discovered, no certainty that the door will open. There was one embarrassing afternoon when we had rung the bell several times and had thereafter, in addition, knocked upon the door very loudly, but still without response, when a very irate voice bellowed from a first floor window on the other side of the alley, 'Who is making that terrible noise at this time of day? Have you no concern for someone who is trying to get some sleep?' Upon which we slunk away, tails between legs, with the leader doing his best to proclaim in dumb show, for the benefit of anyone who might be watching, his version of the old school motto, 'Please, sir, it wasn't me'.

The second particular objective in our Jaffa visit never fails to be a rewarding one. It is a visit to the Church of Scotland's Tabeetha School in the heart of the town. A multiracial, multicultural establishment, it has more than a century of notable achievement to its credit and, despite the difficulties peculiar to the modern situation in Israel, it is still a potent force in the community.

Tabeetha School was founded in remarkable fashion. In 1963 a young Scots woman, Jane Walker-Arnott by name, suffering from poor health, came out to the dry climate of the Holy Land in hope of eking out a little longer her short expectancy of life. She settled in Jaffa, being then the only European in the town. Before long she felt the urge to help some of the girls in the town by offering them a means of education in a Christian atmosphere. She therefore began a mission for girls which (after the lady of Acts) she called the Tabeetha Mission. This speedily developed until before very long Jane Walker-Arnott found herself the headmistress of a full-blown school. She did indeed end her days there but these days were eked out considerably longer than anticipated or hoped, and it was not until 1911, forty-eight years on and at the age of 75, that her life came to an end. So much did so many owe to her by then that we are told that no less than 3000 mourners attended her funeral.

While her life ended then, her work continued and still does. The Tabeetha School which she founded is still functioning and functioning well. Today it has about 300 pupils, both boys and girls, of many races and many colours, many of whom are embassy children but many, too, are local.

It is a refreshing experience to spend an hour in the school. The children invariably send us on our way having succeeded, without even trying, in lifting up our hearts to great heights. The usual pattern of our visit is that the head teacher gives us a brief word about the origin, history and present life of the school and then, divided into groups, we are distributed around various classes. There we see something of what the children are about and probably listen as they sing us a song or a hymn. That is always a joy but before we reach that stage we are likely to have a mutual introduction session which is just as much of a joy. One after another the youngsters stand up and tell us their names and where they come from. In every class there are sure to be about a dozen different countries represented. We greatly enjoy hearing them introduce themselves in this way and they appear to enjoy doing it. Even more, however, they enjoy hearing these (strange?) visitors tell

119

them who they are, where they come from and what they do.

Across the bay from Jaffa lies the large modern city of Tel Aviv which did not even exist at the beginning of this century. The century was well begun before Tel Aviv was born and for quite a time it was counted as no more than a suburb of Jaffa. North of Jaffa at the beginning of the twentieth century was simply uninhabited sand. In 1909 some of the minority Jewish population of Jaffa bought an area of these sand dunes for the purpose of building for themselves some better housing of a more European style than the Arab-type dwellings they had in Jaffa. They called their new development Tel Aviv which means Hill of Spring, and although temporarily interrupted by the First World War, it steadily grew until in 1921 it officially ceased to be a suburb of Jaffa when it was granted a charter that turned it into a town in its own right. Now it is the busiest city in Israel.

From Jerusalem to Galilee

$\mathbf{T}$hose who lead pilgrimages to the Holy Land are divided in their opinion about whether it is better to 'do' Jerusalem or to 'do' Galilee first. Most such pilgrimages are two-centre affairs, spending perhaps eight nights in Jerusalem and six nights in Tiberias. Without any doubt the Jerusalem part of the tour is much the more demanding physically and probably also emotionally for this is the area where there are many more sites to visit and many more miles to travel. Some leaders, therefore, feel that it is better to have the less demanding Galilee part of the tour first, let the pilgrims become acclimatised to the various aspects of the pilgrimage in a more leisurely way and then move on to the faster pace required in the Jerusalem area. Others feel it is preferable to undertake the more crowded - physically and spiritually - experience first and then to be able to relax in the less hectic second stage with time and opportunity to digest and reflect.

I belong to the 'Jerusalem first' school. I have tried it both ways and I know that either has a great deal to commend it. On balance, however, I reckon that it makes for an even more enjoyable and enriching pilgrimage to consume the larger course of the feast first.

Part of our pilgrimage nowadays, therefore, is the journey north from Jerusalem to Galilee on the day of transit from stage one to stage two. It is not just a matter of moving self and baggage from one hotel to another; it is a pilgrimage day in its own right. Although it is not the only route to Galilee, I normally choose that we journey through Samaria, as Jesus chose to do on a notable occasion recorded in St John's Gospel, chapter 4. This route takes us to within sight of a number of biblically significant places.

Before we come to any of them we have our leavetaking of Jerusalem. This is understandably a somewhat emotional moment for most of the party as they have come to love the Holy City for itself as well as for its Christian associations. But it helps to have such a magnificent panorama of the city as is given us for our final view of it when the bus traverses Mount Scopus at the beginning of its journey north. It looks superb in the glow of the morning sun. As we head across Mount Scopus bound for Samaria and Galilee, we are able to see something of the new building that has gone on apace since the Israelis reoccupied the area subsequent to the Six Days' War - the new University Campus, for instance, the new broadcasting station and a number of new hotels. Amid the newness we usually take a few minutes for reflection on the past as we stop at the British War Cemetery, where the rows of graves in their orderly, well-kept plots tug at many heartstrings as we look on them sleeping quietly in sight and sound of the Holy City.

As we proceed on our journey we pass through the village of Sha-Afat (or Shufat) which is adjacent to the remains of biblical Gibeah, the capital city of King Saul. Shortly afterwards we pass by the site of another well-known Old Testament place, Mizpeh. When we come to Bireh (Beeroth of the Old Testament) some eight miles out of Jerusalem, we have reached the place where, so the tradition runs, Joseph and Mary discovered that their twelve-year-old first born, Jesus, was not with the caravan and had presumably been left behind in Jerusalem. (Luke 2: 41ff).

It was customary, essential almost, that when people from distant towns and villages planned to travel to Jerusalem for one of the great festivals, they got together to form a long caravan of fellow-travellers. The young people would often be with their contemporaries and not with their parents. That is no doubt how it came about that Jesus's absence was not noticed until the caravan made its first stop out of Jerusalem which was, as always, at Bireh.

Not much further north we pass close by an Arab village called Beitin which itself is just beside the site of Bethel where Jacob had his remarkable dream (Genesis 28:12-18). There is a tradition that the stone set under the seat of the Coronation Chair in Westminster Abbey is the very same stone - Jacob's Pillow - on which Jacob's head rested when he had his famous dream. But then, there are some who would dispute that the stone presently under the Coronation Chair is the original Coronation Stone - but that is quite another story.

From this point a picturesque route takes us over the heights of the Mountains of Samaria and brings us after a while to a roadside cafe-shop which provides a spectacular viewing point of the colourfully beautiful valley of Libbona spread out below. We can see clearly, too, from this point the serpentine road which is shortly to take us down the hillside and through the verdant fruitfulness of the valley itself.

By this time we are not far from Jacob's Well which is the first major visit of our day's touring. This is one of the best authenticated ancient sites in the

Holy Land - indeed, there may well be none that is better authenticated in the whole world. Here we have beyond any doubt the very same well as that one beside which Jesus had a most dramatic conversation with a Samaritan woman (John 4) one hot summer's day.

Nowadays the well-head is considerably below ground level and we have to descent a flight of steps to get to it. Since the fourth century, more than one church has been built over it and in 1914 the site was cleared yet again preparatory to the erection of a new church over the well. This was to be a magnificent edifice (Greek Orthodox) but money ran out when only the perimeter walls had been completed. That was how things remained for more than seventy years but building work resumed in 1987.

The well-head, which would be at ground level in Jesus' time, was enclosed in the crypt of the first church built on the site and is so enclosed to this day. We find it in the middle of the crypt chapel which has been built over and around it. A low stone parapet surrounds it and on the parapet is a metal bucket, attached to rope and windlass. When we look down into the well we can catch just the faintest glint of water because it is so far below. The well, in fact, is more than 100 feet deep.

It takes a long time for the rope to be paid out far enough for the bucket to reach the water and, when it does, it looks scarcely any bigger than a five pence piece glistening so far below. After the bucket enters the water and fills up, we haul it (laboriously!) back to the surface and most of the group have a drink, in somewhat awed awareness that they are drinking from the same well as once supplied Jesus with a cool drink on a hot day.

All this makes it much more meaningful when we gather in the shade above and read the Gospel story of Jesus' encounter with the Samaritan woman at this very well-head. Not that it is always a straightforward matter of arriving at Jacob's Well, taking my group down the stairs, showing them the well and taking them back up again.

Sometimes we have to wait, if other groups are ahead of us - and on one occasion we had to wait a very long time, because we found ourselves preceded by a group of 500 Greek Cypriot Women. These women were all elderly, all dressed in black and all very devout. When we arrived, about 200 of them had still to visit the well itself. There they were, in a long black line, waiting their turn to go down the steps at one side of the crypt when enough had come up the steps at the other side to make space for them.

Our time schedule is always a bit tight but sometimes delays are inevitable and have to be accepted with as good grace as possible. This was one such because it would have been unthinkable to bypass a visit to the well itself. So we waited in the sunshine until at last the crypt was nearly clear of the Greek Cypriot women and we could go down.

Travels in the Holy Land

We found the floor awash with well water, ankle-deep, and we soon saw the reason for it. The Greek women still within the crypt were all filling little narrow-necked containers with water from the well, as presumably all the rest of the group had done before them. But they were transferring the water from the bucket to their containers, not by dipping the container into the bucket and filling it that way, but by pouring the water over its neck. The result was that much more water ended up on the floor of the crypt than ended up in the containers.

We came across the same group two days later. They were - all of them - being baptised by immersion in the River Jordan at the point where it leaves the Sea of Galilee to flow on south. They were dressed still in their unrelieved black. They presented a somewhat bizarre sight and yet a touchingly lovely one, too, for they were so patently and sincerely devout.

Jacob's Well is at the southern tip of the city of Nablus which is the modern version of the ancient biblical city of Shechem. Nablus is situated between two mountains. On one side is Mount Gerizim, 2848 feet above sea-level, and on the other side is Mount Ebal, 3077 above sea-level, both of which feature in Old Testament history.

Nablus is of great interest to Christian pilgrims not only because it contains Jacob's Well but also because it contains a community of Samaritans. The Samaritans are a diminishing race. Only about four hundred still survive, most of whom live together in Nablus with a much smaller group in Holon, near Tel Aviv. It is surely ironical that the numbers of the Samaritans have fallen so low mainly on account of their practice of inbreeding, which is the result of an uncompromising exclusiveness which prohibits them from marrying outside their own sect. The irony is that the great antipathy the Jews held for the Samaritans after the exile was because the Samaritans, during the exile, had failed to be exclusive but instead had intermarried with their foreign overlords.

This small community of Samaritans in Nablus is located in that part of the city which is built on the slopes of Mount Gerizim. They are very welcoming to visitors and are very willing, eager one might say, to display their most treasured possession, a very old parchment copy of the Pentateuch which they claim is the oldest book in the world. Be that as it may, there is no doubt that it is an extremely valuable document as well as being very old and it is quite fascinating to have the priests bring it out for our inspection.

At times of strife or unrest, such as during the *intifada*, discretion dictates that we avoid Nablus, an Arab city on the border between Israel and Jordan as it existed prior to the Six Days' War. Because of its situation and its past involvement, Nablus is almost bound to be affected by any political tension that might be felt in the land; and so it sometimes may be thought wise to omit Nablus (and so, of course, Jacob's Well and the Samaritans) from our itinerary.

Most years, however, I have been able to take my group there - and never did we meet any trouble in so doing. I went, for instance, on my very first visit to the Holy Land after the Six Days' War and that had an interesting sidelight to it. Having been only twice previously to the Samaritan synagogue I had only a very rough notion of how to get to it; and our driver was equally vague.

Accordingly, when we drove into the main street of Nablus, he stopped the bus and hailed a young boy who was passing along to ask if he could give us directions. The driver and the boy had a long conversation but, since it was conducted entirely in Arabic, I knew nothing of what was being said. When at last the conversation came to an end and the driver, with a smile and a wave, took farewell of the lad, I asked, 'Was he able to give you directions in the end?'

'Oh, yes', replied the driver, 'but that did not take up much time. The reason that we talked so long was that he remembered me from the war last year. I was a tank commander and I was the first Israeli soldier to enter Nablus when we conquered and occupied it. That boy saw me riding in on my tank then and today he recognised me.'

'Has he seen you again before today?' I asked and my driver said 'No'. 'That means', I went on, 'that, although he had seen you only once before and that was a year ago, when you were in uniform, he still knew you immediately. That's a fantastic feat of memory.'

'Yes, it is' the driver replied. 'But it is not unusual. Jews and Arabs have very, very good memories.'

I was reminded of boarding the launch at Capernaum in 1967. This was only my second tour and two years had gone by since my first. When I stepped on board the launch, the young crewman who was handing us aboard, said to me, 'Welcome back'. I said in some surprise, 'How did you know I had been here before?' 'Because' he replied, 'I remember you sailing on my launch two years ago'.

Apart from anything else, these evidences of tremendous powers of memory regularly exhibited by the middle-eastern races, phenomenal by western standards, serve to strengthen my conviction that in the decades when the Gospel tradition was mainly in oral form, its accurate preservation was assured.

It is just a short run of nine miles from Nablus to the ancient city of Samaria. The bus leaves the main road and makes a steep ascent before creeping through the narrow streets of the Arab village of Sebastia to arrive almost at the top of an eminence which dominates the whole of the surrounding area and affords a spectacular view of the plain below and the mountains of Samaria beyond. Here was where King Omri chose to build his Capital city in 876 BC. He built right on the top of the mountain so that the city commanded the entire district for miles around. His son Ahab expanded the city and the excavations made earlier this century have revealed among other things the foundations of the palaces of these two kings.

Samaria suffered much in the Assyrian conquest of the land and in subsequent centuries it was variously destroyed and rebuilt before it was handed over to Herod the Great in 30 BC by the Roman Emperor. Herod rebuilt the city in his usual splendid style and in honour of the Emperor he renamed it Sebaste (Greek for Augustus), a name retained in the present day by the village built just below the ruins of the ancient city.

An early Christian tradition arose to the effect that it was here at Samaria that John the Baptist was beheaded after the notorious dance by Salome. I often refer to this as I begin to lead my group on a walk round the excavated ruins and I tell them that, in order to make the story more vivid, I will invite the youngest female member of the party to perform before us her version of 'The Dance of the Seven Veils'. So far I have never had anyone take me up on my invitation.

Usually during our visit to Samaria I take my group for lunch to Rajab's Restaurant. It lies in the heart of the village and is not at all pretentious - rather unprepossessing in appearance if the truth be told. But the Arab meal Rajab provides is always marvellously acclaimed and we have a lot of fun as, at the conclusion of the meal, he bedecks a number of the group in exotic Arab costumes.

There was some additional entertainment on my last visit when Rajab informed me that his 94-year-old chef had lost his wife the previous year and now felt it was time to replace her. I, in turn, informed the group that they could, if they cared, offer themselves for inspection as possible candidates for the position. I was greatly touched when all the lady members declared that they would much prefer to continue in my company.

I solemnly thanked them for their loyalty to me and told them that as a reward I would show them another interesting ancient site by taking them to Megiddo. Megiddo lies at the opposite end of the Valley of Jezreel from Samaria. It has a known history that reaches back into the mists of time and most of its history has a military connotation.

This is because of its situation. For many centuries it was a place of great strategic importance because it lay at the opening of the most important pass on the great highway, called the Way of the Sea, which connected Egypt with Assyria. This meant that it occupied a controlling position in relation to the great traffic both of armies and of traders that had to pass along this route.

It is known to have been a fortified city even before 3000 BC and in succeeding centuries it often found its way into historical records. It is mentioned, for instance, in ancient Egyptian writings. The Pharaoh Thutmose III attacked it in 1478 BC and an account of the battle is recorded on the walls of the Temple of Karnak in Upper Egypt. It is mentioned a number of times in the Old Testament. It was, for instance, fortified by King Solomon and a number of important battles were fought here, as the Bible records tell us. Although Megiddo lost a lot of its importance long before the Christian era, it had already acquired a lasting reputation as a symbol of war and when the Book of Revelation looks ahead to the last great battle that will usher in the end of the world, it foresees it as taking place at Megiddo. It actually speaks of the place of the final conflict as Armageddon which is really 'Har Mageddon' meaning 'the hill of Megiddo'.

A big archaeological 'dig' on the site in 1925 uncovered a considerable amount of the ancient city, with had been uninhabited since the fourth century. Prominent among the remains brought to light are the round Canaanite altar which is to be dated about 2000 years before the birth of Jesus but is marvellously well preserved, and the equally well preserved large grain silo which is dated about the ninth century BC.

Perhaps the most fascinating 'relic' to be seen on Megiddo is the underground tunnel which was constructed in order to ensure that in any time of siege the city's water supply would be secure. Situated at the southern end of the mound, the Water Tunnel is cut through the rock of the hillside at a depth of nearly 200 feet. It is reached by descending nearly 200 steps which take us quite steeply from the Tel above to the passageway below. This is not a water channel like Hezekiah's Tunnel in Jerusalem. It was constructed as a hidden, underground approach to the spring outside the city which was its main source of water. As a result, we are able in this instance to walk along the tunnel in quite normal fashion and without getting our feet wet.

For most pilgrims the highlight of this transit day of travel and of site-visiting is still to come - their first glimpse of the Sea of Galilee.

Tiberias, our destination, is built beside that Sea, which is, surely to every eye, a superbly beautiful stretch of water, especially so with its exquisite shade of blue highlighted by the afternoon sun. This is how we see it as we approach it from Megiddo, sweeping round a bend in the road and suddenly catching sight of it spread out below us like a carpet.

The Sea of Galilee has several names. It is also called Lake Galilee, the Sea of Tiberias, Gennesaret. The Jews often refer to it as Lake Kinneret. Kinneret literally means 'like a harp' and this name is given alternative explanations.

Travels in the Holy Land

Some maintain that it simply indicates that the sea is harp-shaped; but another and more romantic suggestion is that it is because the sound of the waves lapping gently on its shore is reminiscent of the sound of a harp.

The Sea of Galilee, nearly 700 feet below the level of the Mediterranean, is 13 miles long, has a greatest width of 9 miles, a greatest depth of 160 feet and its shoreline has a total length of 32½ miles. Fed mainly by the River Jordan, it is a freshwater lake.

For a number of successive years in the 1970s there was a steady drop in the level of the Sea of Galilee. This was due to a corresponding succession of lower than usual winter rainfalls allied to a controversial government policy of piping water south from the lake to the Negev desert for the purposes of irrigation.

One exciting consequence of this was that in January 1986 the level of the sea had fallen so abnormally low that stretches of seabed were exposed that had been hidden from view since before the time of Jesus; and this revealed the remains of a boat of the first Christian century embedded in the seabed clay. This was on the north-west coast, a handful of miles from Tiberias and close to the kibbutz guest-house of Nof Ginnosar.

Fortunately the clay in which the boat was embedded had preserved it wonderfully well throughout all these centuries. In a painstaking operation reminiscent of the salvage of the Mary Rose - although of necessity carried through much more speedily - the boat was recovered from its seabed home. It is now on display in a preservative tank in the grounds of Nof Ginnosar and allows us to see the kind of vessel that sailed on the Sea of Galilee in Jesus' day.

Boats still sail on that sea and there is still a lot of fishing done. The boats, it need hardly be said, are a good bit different from what they were. Most of them are motorised for one thing and it is by motor launch that I take my groups 'sailing' on the Sea of Galilee. This, for most Christian pilgrims, probably for all, is one of the most memorable experiences of their entire pilgrimage.

Partly this is because they feel with such certainty that they are where Jesus often was, seeing very much the same picture as he did then. Many things and many places in the Holy Land have suffered change since Jesus was there. Inevitable although that is, many people are disappointed that it should be so. Unreasonable it may be, but they would like everything to be just as it was in his time.

The Sea of Galilee, however, is much as it was when Jesus sailed its waters and so are the hills that surround it. It is, then, a marvellous feeling to be sailing on the sea that he sailed on so often and to look out from the boat to the land in the sure knowledge that we are looking on much the same scene as he often saw.

From Jerusalem to Galilee

The most memorable part of a memorable experience usually comes when, at my request, the Captain cuts the engine part of the way across the sea and allows us to drift gently (or sometimes not quite so gently, if there is a bit of a wind). While we drift, I read the Gospel narrative of how Jesus calmed the storm which was terrifying his disciples on the bosom of this very sea.

It may be difficult to imagine when one is there in spring or summer, but storms frequently do arise on the Sea of Galilee. Sometimes these storms can come very suddenly and at times be very fierce. Their suddenness and their ferocity have something to do with the surrounding terrain and, in particular, with the various gullies and ravines that are dotted around. One minute it can be perfectly calm and the next, especially in winter, a raging tempest.

It was just such a storm as that which caught Jesus and his disciples in their boat in the Gospel narrative I read to my groups. In their panic the disciples woke up Jesus who was asleep in the stern and he at once stilled both the storm and their fears. As we are reminded of this dramatic incident, on the selfsame sea where it happened, we are reminded, too, that, whatever storms of life we may have to sail through, Jesus is willing to sail with us and calm our fears.

Tiberias

In the time of Jesus there were many towns and villages populating the Sea of Galilee coastline, but today Tiberias is the only populated place on its shores apart from kibbutzim. Situated about the midway point on its western shore, Tiberias is where most Holy Land groups stay for the Galilee part of their tour.

Tiberias was a new town in 20 AD, built by Herod Antipas on the ruins of an old one and named in honour of the Emperor Tiberius. It lies 682 feet below sea level; hot in summer, warm in winter, it is a large and steadily expanding holiday resort and almost entirely Jewish.

We have no knowledge of Jesus ever having any personal association with Tiberias but it is a good place for Christian pilgrims to stay because it is within easy distance of many Bible sites. It is also pleasant to live in and interesting in its own right. One place of considerable interest is the Church of Scotland Centre.

More than a century ago a young Christian doctor, called David Torrance, went out to Galilee from his home town of Airdrie in Scotland in order to engage in missionary work under the auspices of his church. After he had spent some time looking around, he came to the conclusion that the need was greatest in Tiberias, right on the lakeside, where the people were very prone to diseases such as malaria, dysentery and cholera.

He met with considerable hostility and much active opposition to begin with, but he persevered and gradually his compassion and his medical skill won him the respect and trust of the majority of the population. The upshot was that he spent practically all of the rest of his life serving the people of Tiberias and district. The cost, however, was agonisingly high to him in personal terms for the disease-ridden conditions in which he was for the most part living and working led to his burying two young wives and three small children there.

130

In 1894, having acquired a stretch of land that ran all the way down to the sea, he was at last able to fulfil a long-cherished ambition and build a hospital to aid him in his work. From then on it was in the hospital that most of his work was done. He died in 1923 and is buried in the little garden cemetery close to the sea, beside his wives and children.

After his death, the work he had founded continued under the leadership of his son, Herbert, now also qualified as a doctor, and it was carried on well into the 1950s. But with the coming into being of the State of Israel in 1948, the end was in sight for the Scottish hospital. Understandably, the Israeli government wished to provide their own hospital service and when, in due course, it built a large, new hospital a few miles from Tiberias, David Torrance's hospital became superfluous.

Church committees are often the object of criticism - sometimes, it must be said, with justification - but in this instance the Church of Scotland committee concerned acted with wisdom and foresight, and perhaps with a bit of courage as well. Instead of shutting up shop altogether in Tiberias, as it might well have been expected to do, it converted the hospital buildings into a tourist guesthouse. This change of use has proved a tremendous boon to very many travellers from many countries. It is there, for instance, that I usually take my pilgrimage groups nowadays.

Occasionally, however, in earlier years we have been accommodated in one or other of the hotels that abound in Tiberias and whose number increases by the year. It was while staying in one of these that I had the experience befall me which every Holy Land leader dreads might happen to him. One of my group died.

We learned later from one of his work colleagues that David Jeffrey had been suffering chest pains for some weeks previously while making his daily walk to work. But he had neither consulted his doctor nor told his wife. He and his wife had both been with me already on a Holy Land tour and had enjoyed it immensely. I often wonder if David was determined not to run the risk of having the doctor advise him to withdraw from the tour; but we will never know.

We were nearing the end of our stay in the Holy Land when it happened. We were due to fly home on the Monday and on the Friday morning David complained of feeling unwell. 'Nothing serious', he said, but he decided he would stay in bed that day rather than join us on the excursion we were to make.

On our return he appeared to be no worse, if no better, and he said he felt able to eat some dinner which, accordingly, I arranged to be sent to his room. Partway through our meal in the dining room, his wife, Rosa, went upstairs to see how he was faring. She was back again very quickly, ashen-faced, to say to me, 'Mr Martin, I think David is dead'.

Travels in the Holy Land

She had found him lying in a heap in the bathroom. I wanted to disbelieve her but rushed upstairs immediately, taking with me a medical doctor who was in the group, and indeed David *was* dead. In addition to the intense sadness of David's death, what followed was perhaps the most bizarre series of events with which I have ever been personally associated.

To begin with, when I went to the hotel manager with the news, his overriding concern was that we should keep knowledge of the tragedy from the other guests. For his hotel to be known to house a dead body would render it ritually unclean according to Jewish religious law, he said, and all his Jewish guests would leave as soon as they knew of it. Not only so, others would avoid it for a considerable period of time. We must somehow, he insisted, remove the body from the hotel secretly under cover of night.

The next problem was the police enquiry. The manager had, as he must, informed the police at once and with this being a sudden death, and of an alien at that, the Chief of Police himself came to the hotel to see to the matter. Unfortunately, he spoke no English, I spoke no Hebrew, the hotel manager's English was fractured and Rosa Jeffrey was hard of hearing. What ensued, therefore, was three hours of an exhausting four-way conversation in the manager's office which, had it not been so heartbreakingly serious, would have had the makings of an hilarious Whitehall farce.

The Chief of Police would ask a question in Hebrew, the manager relayed it to me in the best English equivalent he could muster, I bellowed my revision of his English into Rosa's ear; and when she answered, the whole process was reversed. This went on - at a very slow rate of progress - until Hugh Kerr, the minister of the Church of Scotland in Tiberias, appeared on the scene. I had telephoned his manse immediately the death occurred and, when I found he was not at home, had left a message. As soon as he returned, he came to the hotel and Hugh spoke fluent Hebrew.

So far as the police enquiry was concerned, things accelerated markedly after Hugh's advent; but they did not yet bring us to the conclusion we wanted, in one very important respect at least. Rosa had decided that she would like to have David buried in the Holy Land. She was sure that this would have been his wish since he had loved it so much; and she had asked me if I could arrange for this to be done.

The Chief of Police, however, insisted that there was no possibility of a burial being sanctioned earlier than Monday, our supposed day of departure. Mainly this was because it was now the Sabbath (Sabbath running from 6 pm Friday to 6 pm Saturday). No one, he maintained, would be available to sign the death certificate before Monday morning, even if all other requirements could be met.

It was a long, hard night which included, among other things, waking British Embassy staff in Tel Aviv at an unearthly hour, but at the end of it, it appeared most unlikely that we could get clearance for the funeral before Monday and I was preparing myself for the probability of staying on with Rosa while the others flew home. The Chief, however, assured us he would do his best to find a solution and advised us to make provisional arrangements for the funeral to take place on the Saturday afternoon, in what seemed a rather vain hope that he might succeed.

There was still the question of removing David's body from his hotel room to the hospital mortuary outside the town and doing so, as the manager demanded, in utter secrecy. Accordingly, at two o'clock in the morning, when the rest of the hotel guests and staff were long abed and the Chief of Police had departed, four of us gathered in the room where David Jeffrey's body lay. Besides myself there were the hotel manager, a young male (non-religious) member of his staff and the doctor who was in my group.

What happened next was like a bad dream. The mortuary van had come from the hospital and was waiting in the yard at the back of the hotel for us to transfer the body in clandestine fashion to it. For one like me with no great muscular strength this was a daunting enough prospect in itself; but the task was to be made even more difficult by the hotel manager. Before he would allow us to commence our sombre task, he insisted on turning off the electricity master switch so that the entire operation of our carrying the corpse of a big, heavy man down two flights of stairs had to be accomplished in pitch darkness.

Several times on the way down the stairs I was sure that another death or at least a severe injury was going to be the outcome of this preposterous charade. Eventually, however, we succeeded without mishap and David was taken away to rest in the mortuary.

In the morning Hugh and I - Hugh in the main, thank God for him - made the arrangements necessary for the funeral to take place that afternoon, although neither of us had any real hope that the required clearance would be obtained. The arrangements involved having a coffin made in Nazareth since no such facilities existed in Tiberias, Jewish town that it is; transport being organised to bring it to the hospital if and when the go-ahead was given; and a grave being dug in the little Christian cemetery a couple of miles north of Tiberias close to the sea. The cemetery, scraped painstakingly out of the hillside, commands a superb view of the Sea of Galilee.

It had just gone noon when Hugh telephoned me to say that the Chief of Police, who had appeared so obdurate the night before, had been marvellously helpful in the end. Against all the odds he had managed to obtain the certification needed and with it permission to bury our dead friend.

At once I telephoned by wife back in Glasgow to pass on the sad news and at the same time to ask her to break it as gently as possible to the Jeffrey son and daughter. She was also to let them know the hour of the funeral so that they might be able to be with us to some small degree, in mind and heart, even though separated by such a volume of miles.

I myself conducted the simple service in the plain, unadorned building which is St Andrew's-by-the-sea Church of Scotland in Tiberias. Rosa wanted it that way. She and David were both staunch members of my congregation of High Carntyne in Glasgow. After the service we buried him in the cemetery and there his body rests, overlooking a scene which he had greatly loved.

That night, after dinner, I told the group that on the next day we would resume our planned programme. It seemed the wisest thing to do and all agreed. At that point came one of the most moving speeches I have ever heard, although one of the shortest. With tears in her eyes and in her voice, Rosa stood up and said, 'Thank you, Mr Martin and thank you, friends, for the wonderful support you have given me'.

That was an experience which will always live with me. So will another of a quite different kind which came to me when I was also quartered in one of the hotels in the upper reaches of Tiberias. On this occasion I was acting as leader to two groups. My own group of some thirty people was in one hotel. A second group of nine, whose intended leader had dropped out shortly before departure, had been assigned to my care at the last minute and they were located in another hotel which was in the same area but some twenty minutes' brisk walk away.

My practice was, at the end of the day's touring, to drop off my own group at our hotel, accompany the other group to theirs, spend half an hour with them over a cup of tea and then walk back to spend the evening with my own group. On the Saturday evening of our stay in Tiberias we returned from an excursion around 5.30 pm and found the whole upper town like a place asleep, with the streets and parks completely deserted. This was because of its being the Jewish Sabbath which, remember, extends from 6 pm Friday to 6 pm Saturday. Half an hour later when I walked back to my own hotel the transformation was breathtakingly spectacular. The streets and the parks were thronged with animated adults and laughing children. It seemed clear that the bulk of the population had been assembled behind their closed doors waiting for the close of Sabbath to allow them to spill out into the open for an evening of fun and recreation.

There was very little fun for the two chiefly concerned in another incident which occurred when my group and I were ensconced in Tiberias in a hotel other than the Scottish Centre. They were two ladies sharing a room. One of the two wore contact lenses and on our first night there, she put them into a glass of water for overnight safe keeping. Her friend meantime filled herself a glass of water in case she should feel thirsty during the night. She did in fact wake up feeling thirsty but got up and quaffed the wrong glass - contact lenses and all.

Genuinely sorry though we all were at what was a most unfortunate mishap, we could not help speculating about the reaction in the insurance company's office when the claim form was received stating, 'The reason for losing my contact lenses was that my friend drank them'.

For many years now I have spent my Tiberias week in the Scottish Centre, which may lack some of the refinements of the new hotels but more than makes up for that in other regards such as its situation and its atmosphere. Not the least of its assets is its proximity to the lakeside. One of the delights of our stay is to be able after a day's touring to stroll along the seafront once dinner is over and then to sit for a spell at one of the waterside cafes, absorbing the sound of the waves lapping softly against the seawall at our feet and of the fish splashing gently back into the water after rising to feed.

The fact that the Scots' Hospice has its own little stretch of beach is also a boon, particularly since it is so close. On one occasion this led to a quite unexpected additional joy. A lady in the group informed me that she had never been baptised and asked me if I would baptise her - by immersion - in the Sea of Galilee. I agreed and the ceremony was conducted on our Sunday morning in Tiberias. It was a perfect morning as a small number of us gathered in the seclusion of the Church of Scotland beach just after seven o'clock. While the others stayed on the shore, Madge and I waded out chest-deep into the warm water. I had never before baptised anyone by immersion and the possible physical difficulties of carrying through the actual baptising part smoothly and with dignity had kept me awake most of the night. In the event everything went marvellously well and that baptismal service in the Sea of Galilee remains one of my most memorable.

The Communion services I have conducted in the gardens of the Scottish Centre have all been memorable events, too. It is my invariable practice to have one such service on every visit and its setting beside that very special sea ensures its memorableness for all concerned - celebrant, assisting elders, congregation.

Strangely enough, the Communion service in the Scottish Centre grounds which I am likely to remember best and most is the only one which I did not conduct myself. I always conduct the service with my back to the sea so that my little congregation will face out across its waters all the time the service proceeds. One year when I had a smallish group and only one cleric in it, Grant Anderson, a retired Church of Scotland minister, I thought he might appreciate the opportunity to celebrate the sacrament in that place and I

135

invited him to do so, which he did. This meant that I, for a change, was facing the sea. The service took place in the late afternoon and as it proceeded, the sun set. The colours across the sea to the Syrian hills on the far shore were an exquisite backdrop to a supremely beautiful service.

Around the Lake

The are many places of interest around the Sea of Galilee and many of these are of religious significance. With the Sea of Galilee being as small as it is and with a road nowadays running all the way round it, all of these places are within easy reach of Tiberias.

Capernaum is to be found almost at the northern extremity of the lake. In the time of Jesus, Capernaum was perhaps the busiest of many busy towns and villages on the Sea of Galilee coastline. Nowadays nearly all of these other places have vanished from sight and Capernaum, once so populous, has no permanent residents except a handful of monks. It does have, however, some striking remains.

Among these is a partially reconstructed synagogue which dominates the present day site. Its date has not yet been positively settled but it is likely to have been built in the third or fourth century AD and certainly it made use of stones from an earlier construction on the same site. The undeniably Roman characteristics of many of these earlier stones make it very likely that they belonged originally to the Capernaum synagogue mentioned in the Gospels which was the gift of a Roman centurion.

Capernaum literally means 'Village of Nahum' but it is not known who this Nahum was. We do know, however, that after having been covered and hidden from sight for many centuries, the ruins of Capernaum were excavated around the end of the nineteenth century by the Franciscans who bought and cleared the site. It was they, too, who made the partial reconstruction of the two-storey synagogue which is to be seen today. Also to be seen are a great number of carved stones from the ruined synagogue and many of these are well worthy of close examination, not only because they illustrate the skill and patience of the craftsmen who carved them but also because of the intrinsic interest of the pictures and symbols that they carved.

137

Travels in the Holy Land

It was not until 1921 that the ruins of dwelling houses were excavated directly in front of the synagogue - on the seaward side. Among these is one over which had been built an octagonal-shaped church dating back to the fifth century. There is clear evidence that there was Christian veneration of this house site from a much earlier time and there is a strong body of belief that here was the home of Simon Peter to which, as the Gospel narratives tell us, Jesus was a frequent visitor. An operation is in hand now - for better or for worse, opinions may vary - to build a modern church on the site.

Just a short distance south, also on the lakeside and, in fact, actually on the water's edge, is a little church called Mensa Christi (The Table of Christ) which is otherwise known as the Primacy of Peter. The church and the two names by which it is known owe their existence to one of the post-Resurrection stories in the Gospels. It is the one which tells of seven of Jesus' disciples fishing on the Sea of Galilee close inshore early one morning when they catch sight of a figure standing on the beach. It is Jesus and when they recognise him and come ashore they all breakfast together.

The spot on which this church has been erected is the one which tradition claimed at an early stage of Christian history as the place where this incident occurred. The present simple church was erected as recently as 1933 AD but vestiges of a fourth-century building on the same site are clearly to be seen still. On the seaward side of the church there are steps cut out of the rock and, while their age cannot be fixed with accuracy, they may well have been cut as early as the second century for the convenience of those arriving at the spot by boat. When Pope Paul VI visited the Holy Land in 1964 and was to visit this church, someone had the happy thought of making it possible for him to enter it directly from the sea. Accordingly, an entrance into the church was made directly above the steps and the Pope came by boat right up to the little stone stair (the water level at that time coming halfway up it) so that he was able to go straight from the boat on to the steps and into the church.

Not a great many yards further south along the shore is the Church of the Multiplication of the Loaves and the Fishes. As its name indicates, this church commemorates Jesus' feeding of the five thousand which he accomplished miraculously with a young lad's picnic lunch of five small loaves and two small fishes. As with nearly every church in the Holy Land, again this one is built on the site of earlier structures. There was a church here in the fourth century which was followed by another erected in the fifth century. The Persians destroyed it in 614 AD and its remains lay hidden for more than thirteen centuries until they were excavated in 1932 AD.

When the excavations were made, a superbly beautiful mosaic floor was exposed to view. It was marvellously well preserved and its colours had survived wonderfully even after nearly 1400 years beneath debris and vegetation. The mosaics represent accurately and vividly, and with great skill, much of the flora and fauna of the region - and the representations are frequently laced with humour, too.

All of these mosaics are set now in the floor along either side of the magnificent church which was built here in the 1980s. The most famous of them is the one which is placed under the altar, depicting five small loaves in a basket, with a fish on either side. This could be said, perhaps, to be a kind of signature for the modern church, as it was for its predecessor.

In the same area but on the crest of the hill overlooking the Sea stands the modern Church of the Beatitudes. Built in 1937 AD, it commands a truly magnificent view of the Sea of Galilee. In this vicinity Jesus gave a great deal of his teaching and preaching, making use of the remarkable open air acoustics.

These acoustics are, as a matter of fact, quite phenomenal. If you stand at the water's edge or wade in a few yards and speak in a normal, conversational tone, you can be heard easily and clearly by someone standing well up the hillside. It is very easy when you are in that spot to visualise Jesus sitting on the shore or in a boat and preaching to hundreds of eager listeners gathered together on the hillside.

That is always for me at least an arresting thought. But invariably I find my most moving experience at the Mount of Beatitudes is when - as I always do - I conduct an open-air Communion service beneath the trees in a corner of the gardens beside the Church. As we have this service, with the Sea of Galilee spread like some opulent carpet of blue below us and with the bird-song accompanying us like some heavenly choir, many hearts are lifted up and many spirits find peace.

There are a number of places in the Holy Land where the Christian pilgrim is likely to be made very conscious that his Lord Jesus is alive. Many find this so around the Sea of Galilee and for some of my pilgrims this is particularly the case on the Mount of Beatitudes during our Communion service. This was so even when on one occasion the sounds of warfare broke in upon our worship. The previous day there had been a guerilla incursion from Lebanon into Israel. At the very moment when we were taking the bread and wine that early morning in obedience to Jesus' command, Israeli warplanes roared overhead bent on a revenge mission, and very soon afterwards we heard the crump of their bombs exploding in Lebanon some forty miles away.

The presence of Jesus was very real to us that morning, despite the poignancy of the occasion, and so were our prayers for the peace of the Holy Land.

The main lakeside sites of Christian significance are concentrated in this

Travels in the Holy Land

small north-eastern area, although the fact that Jesus spent so much of his ministry around its shores makes it inevitable for the Christian pilgrim that the whole expanse of the Sea of Galilee and its surroundings gives eloquent reminder of him. A journey round the circumference of the lake therefore, does not go amiss.

There is much general interest in the course of such a journey. If you start off from Tiberias and travel north, you will shortly see on you left hand side, that is, the west, a long, low hill with a peak at both ends. This is called the Horns of Hittin (or Hattin), so named because of its shape.

This is where Saladin defeated the Crusaders in battle, on 4th July 1187 AD and by so doing brought to an end what was called the Latin Kingdom of the Crusaders with its capital in Jerusalem.

A mile or two further brings us to a mound and a few ruins on the shore side, that is, the right hand side of the road. This is where the Magdala of the New Testament is believed to have been located, the town where the prostitute Mary plied her trade until she found her life changed by meeting with Jesus. Just beyond this point a road branches off to the left. A signpost carries the name Migdal and this small village on the hillside, some distance from the Sea, is what has taken the place and the name of that New Testament Magdala which was a town of considerable size.

By now we are able to see the channel between us and the Sea along which a steady flow of water is sent south from the Sea of Galilee to irrigate the Negev, and very soon we see the pumping station which sends that water on its way. Next we come to the area containing the Church of the Beatitudes, the Church of the Multiplication and the Church of Mensa Christi. This area is called Tabgha which is a corruption of the Greek Heptapegon which means 'Seven Springs.' At one time seven springs fed into the Sea at this point although only five of them have survived to the present day.

Going past Capernaum and round the north end of the lake, we cross the delta of the River Jordan and cross at the same time into what was Syrian territory before the Six Days' War of 1967 but is now occupied by Israel. As we head south on the east coast we come to the ruins of what was a large fifth-century monastery at Kursi, a place which tradition has sometimes identified as the location of the healing of the madman which was accompanied by the stampede of a herd of pigs into the sea.

Only a brief journey from Kursi brings us to the kibbutz of Ein Gev. Many pilgrimage tours make a point of spending a few hours here. Mine always does and it is well worth a visit. It lets us see and hear something of the nature of a kibbutz, a kind of community farm. Ein Gev was founded in 1937, numbers about 400 members and is particularly interesting to visitors because of its situation on the very edge of the Sea of Galilee.

This is not only because of its attractiveness in appearance although there is a lot of that. Created out of what was in the beginning almost total desolation, Ein Gev today presents a picture of pleasant colour and lush vegetation. Nor is it only because of its remarkable concert hall. Built to seat 2000 and possessing outstandingly good acoustics, it regularly stages concerts that feature artistes of international stature such as Yehudi Menuhin and the Israel Philharmonic Orchestra. I am told that on such nights the lights of a myriad of small boats making their way across the Sea of Galilee to Ein Gev make a spectacular sight.

It is also because it existed for many years under the threat of Syrian guns. When the State of Israel was created and the partition of the land was established in 1948, Ein Gev found itself occupying a strip of coastal land that was overlooked and menaced by Syrian guns on the heights above. Periodically, when tension and mistrust erupted into fighting, Ein Gev would find itself a very exposed target and at such times the bomb shelters were used to capacity. It is no wonder that the occupants of Ein Gev felt great relief when the Six Days' War of 1967 led to Israeli occupation of these Syrian heights and the removal of the constant threat of coming under shell-fire.

We used always to have one of the founder members of Ein Gev, Ben Joseph by name, as our guide on a short walking tour of the Kibbutz. A man of great erudition and also of great compassion, his explanations of kibbutz life in general and of Ein Gev in particular were delightful as well as informative. He always concluded our tour by taking us into the vast auditorium of the concert hall and, when he was finished, he asked us to sing 'The Lord's my Shepherd' to the tune Crimond.

In the mid-1980s, following a severe illness, he became noticeably frail but he continued to guide our pilgrim groups round the kibbutz. When I visited in the spring of 1987, his voice, once so strong and firm, had become so weak that at times we could barely make him out above the singing of his beloved *bulbuls* (Turkish nightingales). When I went back with a group in late November of that same year, I was met with the sad news that Ben Joseph had died just a few days before. The kibbutz was in process of preparing a Book of Memory in his honour and I was moved and grateful to accept the invitation to be the first to enter my tribute in it.

At the southern extremity of the lake stands kibbutz Degania founded in 1912, the earliest of these collective settlements to come into existence. It was very much an experimental enterprise. The area was quite barren and swamp-ridden. The original settlers were not only working in a tropical climate and constantly liable to attack from hunting Bedouin tribesmen, but they had come with very little expertise in agriculture. The early years were, therefore, almost inevitably attended by many failures and frustrations. However, they persevered and, learning much by trial and error, they have not only produced a lovely and fertile settlement but in it have provided a pattern for other kibbutzniks. Degania is also a place that, like Ein Gev, gives constant thanks for the change in its circumstances brought about by the Six Days' War. Until then it was in a very vulnerable position, being located virtually on the border of three countries - Israel, Jordan and Syria - and since hostilities not infrequently erupted between the other two and Israel, Degania was apt to find itself caught in a three-way crossfire.

It is just beside Degania that the River Jordan leaves the Sea of Galilee to flow south to the Dead Sea. On occasion I have found time to stop briefly here so that those of the group so minded could swim in and across the River Jordan. It is always quite a thrill to do just that.

From Degania we head north back to Tiberias but just a mile and half before we reach the town, we come upon the Hot Springs, whose fame goes back to antiquity. Here we can see the spring water spilling out of the ground boiling hot and bearing a strong sulphur smell. Centuries before Christ these springs were well-known for their therapeutic qualities, especially with regard to illnesses such as rheumatism and gout. Today thousands come each year to bathe in the Hot Springs waters.

There is an unusual but interesting legend which connects the origin of the Hot Springs with King Solomon. It tells of a group of men suffering from various skin and joint ailments coming to Solomon and pleading with him to find some means of helping them. Solomon, in response to their plea, sent a number of demons to heat the cold water produced by a spring at this very spot. This they did so that the water issuing forth became *hot* water.

The legend continues, 'When the demons began their work, Solomon made them deaf, for he knew well that should news of his death reach them they would no longer fear him and would cease to heat the fountain. Solomon is dead, but the deaf demons not having heard of his death, and thinking that he still lives in his palace in Jerusalem, continue to heat the fountains to this day'.

Nazareth

Nazareth is always one of the places to be visited that Christian pilgrims anticipate with a special degree of excitement. This is not surprising, for this, of course, is where Jesus spent most of his earthly life.

Nazareth did not command much of a reputation in the time of Jesus. As a matter of fact it was the object of some ridicule in a proverb of the day which is quoted by Nathanael in John 1:46, 'Can anything good come out of Nazareth?' This may be hard to understand when Nazareth's geographical position is taken into account. The hills around the town overlook the Valley of Jezreel which was then, as it is now, far and away the most fertile area in the land. It was also one of the great crossroads of the east. Traders and soldiers of many nations regularly passed by here.

Until quite recent times Nazareth was a wholly Arab town, with the majority of its population being Christian and the remainder Moslem. Since 1948 there has been a steadily increasing Jewish population in the new housing in the upper reaches of the town. Today Nazareth is dominated by the towering and magnificent structure of the Church of the Annunciation which stands right at its centre. But when I saw Nazareth first that church was not there.

There had already been several churches built on this site. This was because it was here, according to tradition, there once stood the house in which Mary received the angel's message that she was to bear a very special boy child. The latest of these churches had been erected in 1730 but had been demolished in 1955 in order to make way for a new one.

On my first visit to Nazareth - in 1964 - the new church was still in the process of being built and was not, in fact, completed until 1966. I have seen it many times since then and it becomes no less impressive through familiarity. Viewed from the outside, the Church of the Annunciation has a striking appearance. It is made of a very light-coloured stone which, set as it is in the centre of a town that seems always to be a whirlpool of hustle and bustle, gives an appearance of such freshness as must both soothe and uplift many a heart.

Inside there is even more beauty. The church is built on two levels. The lower church contains the Cave of the Annunciation, that part of the home of Mary which was visited by the angel, and also surviving parts of the Byzantine and Crusader churches which once occupied the site. The lower church is reserved for private masses and special services.

The upper church is the one used for parish worship. Large and full of light and colour, it has many impressive features. Notable among them are the exquisite mosaics from many different countries which are set in panels on the walls on either side. Most impressive of all, perhaps, is the dome. Nazareth literally means 'lily' and the dome has been constructed to represent an open lily upside down with its petals stretching downwards to embrace the congregation. The symbolism is that the love of God, rooted in heaven, reaches down in Jesus to embrace all mankind.

In the courtyard adjoining the lower church there is a series of splendid modern mosaics, gifted from all corners of the globe like those in the upper church. In the courtyard adjoining the upper church there is also a modern-day gift, a magnificent baptistry; but this courtyard has, in addition, something arresting on display that is ancient: below the baptistry part of a Nazareth street of Jesus' own time has been excavated and exposed to view.

On the other side of the courtyard of the upper church is another church, the Church of St Joseph. A tradition has identified this as the site of the combined home and carpenter's workshop of Joseph and so, at a later stage, of Jesus. Certainly there are remains visible beneath the church of such a workshop home but the tradition connecting this with the holy family is very late and there is no known historical evidence to back it up. Nevertheless, it is interesting to visit the church and to descend to the crypt to see the remains of that early house which might well have been, at least, very similar to the one in which Jesus spent his boyhood and early manhood.

One of the additional sources of enjoyment and of pilgrimage profit for many years was to have Ahmed, a local Arab guide, to escort us round the Church of the Annunciation. He was my guide there the first time I led a Holy Land group and I have always sought his assistance in subsequent years. On the very few occasions when he was not available, it was not only a disappointment to me but a loss to the group.

He never used two words where one would suffice but he was both knowledgeable and understanding. He used to mingle his informative guide talk with gems of Christian wisdom and philosophy. Some of his habitual sayings are deeply ingrained in my memory. Habitually, for instance, after having us standing round him for a few minutes as he explained some feature, he would conclude that particular interlude by saying, 'Now, take it easy and follow me' - and set off at a rate of knots which always left at least half of the group floundering some distance in his wake.

Ahmed, I think, had somehow given me the feeling that he was indestructible and unchangeable. It was, therefore, a shock to discover him suddenly turned frail, following a severe illness. When I went looking for him as usual on my last visit and found him standing outside the guides' office beside the church, my heart lifted, 'He's back at work', I said to myself, 'He must be much better. Good'.

'Ahmed', I said, 'It's good to see you again and I would like you as usual to be my guide for the church.'

After he had embraced me in the typical Arab fashion, he said, in a voice that was only a faint echo of what it had been, 'Minister' (that was how he always addressed me) 'Minister, you don't need me today. You can do it better yourself'.

That Ahmed should refuse a guiding job sent a chill through my heart. I knew that he must be feeling very weak to do that. Not just because he was refusing the opportunity to earn some money. That was significant enough. Even more so was the fact that he was rejecting the opportunity to tell people about the church, a task he loved doing.

I hope he will be much restored in health and back on the guiding job again on my next visit - but my hope is not matched by great confidence.

Although the Church of the Annunciation is the dominating feature in Nazareth, both structurally and in most other ways, and the chief attraction for tourists and pilgrims, there are many other features of considerable interest. There are two in particular which my groups always delight in visiting.

One is the hospital of the Edinburgh Medical Missionary Society. For more than a century splendid work has been going on here in Christ's name for the Arabs of the town and district; and even after Israel came into being in 1948, the hospital was allowed to continue its work. Situated high up on the hillside overlooking Nazareth on the west, the Scottish Hospital, as it is often referred to (although the medical and nursing staff are very cosmopolitan), is difficult of access for a large, modern bus. With a co-operative driver, however, the ascent can be made and there is always some member of staff who will take the time and trouble to show us round.

Without fail the maternity section with its very young babies is a source of delight to the ladies in the group, and no doubt to most of the men, also, bravely though they try to hide the fact. But, as with any hospital, there are some patients more likely to cause tears than laughter. One boy has been a patient for the past few years after an horrific road accident which left him totally unable to do anything for himself and only barely conscious at the best of times. Abandoned by his family, the hospital is the only home he will ever have.

When I tell you there is not the remotest chance of any improvement in his physical condition ever being possible, you might well ask if all the time and skill, not to speak of the money, being expended in keeping him alive would not be more wisely and more advantageously spent in other ways. On the face of it there may seem to be only one possible answer. And yet, to have been there is to make me wonder at the same time if such undoubtedly loving care as is bestowed upon that broken body could possibly be regarded by God as a waste.

Year after year I have left that lad's ward without being any closer to knowing what the correct answer should be.

Of particular interest, over and above the hospital itself, is the hospital chapel. Opened and dedicated the very week before my visit to it in 1965, its main supporting structure is in the form of a large stone cross whose arms reach out as if to enfold the town below; and its communion table is in the shape of a carpenter's bench with the work side facing the congregation.

The other additional Nazareth visit which meets with great approval is to the Church of the Adolescent Christ. Even higher up the hillside and even more difficult of access for a bus, it well repays any special effort that may be required to get there. The church is actually the chapel of a school for Arab boys run by the Salesians, a French order founded by Dom Bosco, and it is a truly magnificent building. Its high columns of white stone reflect the sunlight streaming in through the windows and produce an immediate feeling of serenity in almost every pilgrim I take there. But the most striking feature of the church is something else. Above the altar is a very appealing representation in stone of the boy Jesus striding through the fields around Nazareth. It gives a touching and pointed reminder that Jesus is no mere stained glass figure without relevance for ordinary daily living. I have found, too, over the years that with the sun coming through the windows at different angles at different hours of the day, the figure of the boy Jesus is thereby given variations of appearance that may be taken as further reminder that he is a friend for all seasons.

It is usual when visiting Nazareth to visit on the same day the Arab village of Kefar-Kanna. It is less than four miles from Nazareth and is believed to be the Cana-in-Galilee of the Gospel narrative. For my part I normally take my group there on the way to Nazareth from Tiberias which means that we arrive in the freshness of early morning. This makes for a very pleasant stroll through the village.

Buses do not, indeed cannot, drive through Cana's narrow streets. So we have to pile out of the bus on the main road and walk into the heart of the village along the narrow street which bisects it to rejoin the main road further on. In the middle of the village, on either side of the street, stand two churches which commemorate Jesus' miracle of changing water into wine. One is Greek Orthodox and the other is Franciscan. Tradition has it that the Franciscan church is actually built on the site of the house where Jesus performed the miracle.

It must be said that there is no certainty that Kefar-Kanna is to be identified with Cana-in-Galilee and that there is no real ground for believing that the Roman Catholic church marks the place where the miracle took place. What does it matter? To visit there is to be reminded that the same Jesus who changed water into wine to save a wedding hostess's embarrassment can, and often does, change the water of ordinary existence into the wine of life at its best. In visiting the Holy Land it is important always, as I keep telling my groups, to look for the holy thing behind the holy place. What we actually see may well be full of interest and significance in itself but what it represents may be even more so.

Sometimes the incidentals of a visit stick in one's mind for ever. I recall two such experiences I had in Cana.

The first occurred many years ago. I was leading my group from the bus along the narrow street into the centre of the village and the churches. I had reached approximately the halfway point when to my astonishment I met another Church of Scotland minister leading a group in the opposite direction. It was Nevile Davidson, minister of Glasgow Cathedral, and I had not even been aware that he was in the Holy Land at that time. It made for a happy encounter.

The second was more recent. I had no sooner alighted from the bus at the entrance to Cana than I was approached by a young Arab boy who offered to guide us to the church. I thanked him and assured him that I knew the way very well and did not need any assistance. But he insisted and kept insisting, very politely, I may say; and in the end, although convinced that all he was concerned about was a tip, I let him act as our guide rather than be bothered trying to shake him off. To my surprise, however, when we had finished our visit and I offered him some money, he waved it aside, saying, 'No, no. I am a Boy Scout. This is my good deed for today'. His action semed to make the bright morning brighter still.

Another thing we often do on our 'Nazareth day' is to visit Mount Tabor. Mount Tabor stands right in the middle of the Valley of Jezreel, otherwise known as the Plain of Esdraelon, the most fertile area in the whole of Israel. It is by far the highest point in the district and consequently dominates the entire region, being visible from many miles away in every direction.

Not that it is a very high mountain as mountains go, far from it. It stands 1843 feet above sea level, much lower than Jerusalem, for example, which is 2900 feet above. But since the rest of Esdraelon is flat, Tabor towers quite majestically over its surroundings.

It also rises very steeply and this fact ensures that ascending it is an exhilarating experience for most modern-day pilgrims. There is a road going all the way to the top but buses are unable to go any further than about two-thirds of that way. Beyond that point the road becomes too narrow and has a rapid succession of hairpin bends, eighteen in all. It would be impossible for our bus to negotiate the upper third of the road and so when we reach the crucial point, we disembark from it and pack into waiting taxis for the remainder of the ascent.

The ride to the top is positively thrilling as we whirl swiftly round one sharp corner after another. At the same time we obtain a marvellous succession of kaleidoscopic views of the countryside beneath us. As we rise steadily higher and higher, the fields with their growing crops present a fascinating series of colourful patchwork views. Once at the top we find a very fine-looking church built on the very crest of the mountain. The church standing there today is a modern church, completed as recently as 1923, but much older churches once stood on the same site; and remains of the Byzantine and Crusader structures are still to be seen.

Mount Tabor has been a place of Christian pilgrimage from early times. Tradition has long regarded it as the place where the Transfiguration occurred, that remarkable event recorded in the Gospels when, in full view of the three disciples who were with him at the time, Jesus was so transformed in appearance that he seemed to be shining with a dazzling light.

It ought to be admitted that it is probable that the Transfiguration may have taken place not on Mount Tabor but on Mount Hermon. There are several reasons for coming to this conclusion. For one thing, the Bible narrative appears to suggest that the event occurred on a deserted mountain whereas Tabor at that time was quite populous. It was, in fact, a strongly defended strategic point with a fort on its top.

For another thing, the geographical situation of Tabor does not fit in easily with the demands of the story. In the Gospels, the Transfiguration experience comes hard on the heels of the occasion at Caesarea where Peter makes what is often referred to as the 'great confession' and declares to Jesus 'You are the Messiah'. The impression given is that the two incidents must have been close together both in time and in place. Now, Mount Tabor is fifty miles distant from Caesarea Philippi and that would take some time to cover on foot which was the usual mode of travel used by Jesus and his disciples. Mount Hermon, on the other hand, is closely adjacent to Caesarea Philippi.

The tradition favouring Tabor - a long standing one, let it be said - may mean that at an early stage it was selected (in somewhat the same way as royal birthdays are selected) as a suitable mountain for commemorating the Transfiguration and convenient for pilgrims to visit since it was much more easily reached than Hermon.

Mount Hermon, then, is more probably the place where the Transfiguration actually occurred. The event would not have taken place on the very top of the mountain which is no less than 9232 feet high but on one of its lower heights, close by Caesarea Philippi. Nevertheless, I feel nothing amiss in taking my groups to the summit of Tabor and there recalling how Jesus was transfigured. A number of places in the Holy Land are what might be termed 'sites of convenience'. We are not to be too concerned as to whether or not they are historically authentic. It is their message that counts.

And whether or not it actually took place there, Mount Tabor speaks very vividly to its visitors concerning the Transfiguration, not least on account of the magnificent mosaics in the church which depict the story. Before we get to these mosaics, I must tell you, we have to pass by a most unexpected and rather sobering sight. At the side of the gate that admits us to the avenue leading up to the church door is a notice which reads: 'If you are here to pray, you are welcome. If you are here only to look, you are also welcome, but please retain from writing your name upon our walls.' Imagine a warning against graffiti being required in such a holy place!

Despite the cold shower type of shock this notice may give and despite the doubt as to whether or not Tabor is the actual location of the Transfiguration, the basilica on top of the mountain, because of its situation and its tradition and its eloquently lovely mosaics, gives a vivid reminder of the marvellous experience which Peter, James and John shared there with Jesus. Such a marvellous experience it was that they wanted it to go on and on.

They did not want to go back down the mountain but, of course, they could not stay indefinitely. They had to return to the ordinary things of ordinary days. We pilgrims, too, invariably feel reluctance to go back down the mountain; but we, too, must. Often I suggest to my groups that there may be a kind of parable in this. Mountain top experiences are wonderful to have and are to be treasured. They cannot, however, last for ever. We must always, sooner or later, return to the plains and the valleys of life, and whatever they may contain for us. But as Jesus accompanied his disciples down the mountainside that day, so he will accompany everyone willing to have his company. That is perhaps a rather obvious homiletical application of the Transfiguration story but I must confess that it did not fully strike home to me until I visited Mount Tabor.

Mediterranean Places

From Tiberias, particularly with the new and much faster roads of recent years, the Mediterranean coast is within easy reach. Most pilgrim group itineraries allocate at least one day for a visit to northern Israel's Mediterranean coastline. The places usually visited on such a trip are Acre, Haifa and Caesarea.

Little more than an hour and a half's driving takes us from Tiberias to Acre, or Akko, as it is usually called in the Holy Land itself. This is one of the world's most ancient towns, being known to history long before Jesus Christ. The Greeks occupied Akko in their time and so did the Romans after them. Both the Greeks and the Romans called it by its alternative name of Ptolemais which it had been given in honour of Ptolemy II, Pharaoh of Egypt, who ruled Palestine and fortified Akko in 261 BC. It is under this name that it receives its solitary mention in the New Testament (Acts 21:7).

Akko not only has a very long history (its first known mention is in Egyptian hieroglyphics of the nineteenth century BC) but also, like most seaports, a very chequered one. Its chief interest for most Christian pilgrims is its association with the Crusaders, who occupied it for about two centuries and who have left behind an imprint of that occupation which is still clearly to be seen. From the time that it was conquered by Baldwin the First in 1104 AD, Akko was the chief seaport of the Crusaders in the Holy Land.

The Knights Hospitallers, the Knights of St John, established their headquarters in the city and because of that it was renamed 'St Jean d'Acre'. When Saladin defeated the Crusaders at the Horns of Hattin in 1187 AD, the Crusaders surrendered Acre without a fight. But it was recaptured four years later by Richard the Lionheart and remained not only the main port but also the capital of the Crusaders' now reduced Palestinian kingdom until their final defeat and expulsion in 1291 AD.

151

Travels in the Holy Land

For centuries after this Acre lay in ruins. It was the middle of the eighteenth century before it regained any stature but at the end of the century it made a significant contribution to the shaping of world history. This was when it played a decisive part in thwarting the plans of Napoleon Bonaparte for world conquest.

Napoleon had conquered Egypt and now laid siege to Acre with the intention of finding here a gateway through which he could open a route to India and the overthrow of the British Empire. The siege lasted sixty days but Napoleon was beaten off in the end by the Turkish Pasha of Acre and district - Jazzar ('the cuthroat') - with the assistance of a British fleet under the command of Sir Sydney Smith. This signalled the end of Napoleon's dreams of world domination.

There are still parts of the massive Crusader walls to be seen in the old city of Akko and they make for exciting viewing. But easily the most impressive Crusader relic to be seen is the Crypt of St John, so called. It is the largest and most spectacular part of the visible remains of what were the headquarters of the Knights of St John. Directly opposite where the Mosque of Jazzar Pasha now stands, these remains extend over an extensive underground area, the street level today being about twenty-five feet above the Crusader level.

The Crypt of St John, now known to have been the dining room of the Hospitallers, has been excavated only in very recent times. I remember on my first visit there, in 1965, passing along the street when our guide indicated what seemed to be the upper part of a Crusader arch at street level in the wall running alongside. 'They've started to excavate down there' he said, 'It's all filled up just now but they think it's the crypt of the Crusader Church of St John, far below our feet.'

Today all of the accessible remains of what were once the quarters of the Knights Hospitallers are open to visitors and they are well worth seeing. Magnificently vaulted halls lead us to the Crypt, where massive circular stone columns support the infrastructure. From the Crypt/Refectory we follow a secret underground passage which served once as an escape route; and are enabled perhaps in so doing to sniff something of the drama and danger of the Crusader times.

Immediately across the bay from Acre and some fourteen miles by road is the city of Haifa, Israel's chief seaport and its third largest city. As our bus takes us these fourteen miles, we are visually reminded of much Old Testament history for we pass through the Valley of Zevulun and cross the River Kishon where Deborah the prophetess defeated the Canaanites.

We are reminded of much more when we come to Haifa, for Haifa is built on Mount Carmel and Carmel is the mountain of Elijah. It was here that he waged his historic contest with the priests of Baal, and Mount Carmel contains a number of reminiscences of Elijah and his association with the mountain.

Carmel also affords what must surely be one of the world's finest views. From Panorama Road, in the upper reaches of the city and high up on the mountainside, there is the most gorgeous outlook over the gold dome of the Bahai shrine, on to the harbour far below and across the wide crescent of the beautiful Bay of Haifa to Acre in the mistiness of the distant northern extremity of that crescent.

Although Mount Carmel is properly that mountain on which Haifa is built, the Carmel range extends far to the south and all of this range is referred to as 'The Carmel'. The Carmel, in fact, reaches almost as far south as Caesarea which is thirty miles away.

Caesarea (not to be confused with Caesarea Philippi) was an important seaport of Palestine in Jesus' day and we come across it frequently in the Book of Acts. It was at that time the official residence of the Roman governor and it was here that Paul spent two years in prison prior to being shipped to Rome to face trial. It had been created in 22 BC by Herod the Great who named it in honour of the Emperor of Rome, and it continued as the Roman capital in Palestine for half a millenium. After the Romans it fell into disuse and largely into ruin until the Crusaders restored and rebuilt it. The Crusader city was much smaller than the Roman city which had preceded it so many centuries before but the rampart they erected to enclose it still stands today, having survived even the Moslem destruction which followed their expulsion of the Crusaders in 1291 AD.

Most of the archaeological excavations which have been made in and around Caesarea were made within the last half century and they have uncovered much of great interest. One Caesarea relic which they did not discover was the legendary Sacro Catino. This is a glass bowl which was believed to have been used by Jesus at the Last Supper. It was kept in Caesarea until the Crusaders' conquest after which it was removed to Italy. It is now in Genoa.

Among the many objects that *were* uncovered, perhaps the most significant is the 'Pilate stone'. A short distance south of Caesarea a splendid Roman amphitheatre was excavated in 1961 AD (now restored and used regularly for open air concerts) and during the excavations a slab of marble was brought to light, apparently part of a VIP seat, bearing an inscription which speaks of the procuratorship of Pontius Pilate in the reign of Tiberius. This secular testimony to Pilate's governorship in the time of Jesus is of obviously great importance.

The actual stone used to be on view within the walls of Caesarea but it has now been removed for safe keeping to the museum in Jerusalem and a replica has been placed not far inside the entrance gate to the amphitheatre.

I always take my groups a short distance north of Caesarea as well. It is not that I have anything to show them there that is of Christian or even of Old Testament association. But it would be remiss of me, when we are so close, not to let them see the Roman aqueducts. These are massive constructions made by the Romans in the second century AD in order to bring fresh water from the hills into Caesarea. What can be seen today of these structures arising out of the sand is immense but there is so much more still hidden from view.

On one occasion when I took my group to see the aqueducts I found the visit illustrating not only how mankind is capable of remarkable technical achievements but also how it is equally capable of acts of folly that can sometimes have embarrassing consequences. It was a very warm day and despite the notices that said 'Swimming Forbidden', the beach was crowded with bathers. A goodly number of my group pleaded to be allowed to join them for a short time.

Against my better judgment, because I am by nature something of a slave to regulations, I eventually yielded; and so as not to seem standoffish, I said that I would also go swimming. We decided to use the bus as our changing hut - women at the back, men at the front - and soon the bathing party was enjoying itself thoroughly in the waters of the Mediterranean (we had not heard anything in those days about their pollution).

After some fifteen minutes in the water I decided it was time we were getting on our way and so we all left the water and trooped back, dripping wet, to the parking area and our bus cum changing hut - and discovered it was no longer there. Nor was it anywhere to be found. So there we were, clad only in our wet bathing attire, for even our towels had been left in the bus, and beginning to feel the chill as a breeze had sprung up. 'Don't worry', I said, all the time worrying like mad myself, 'The bus will be back in a minute.'

But it was a whole lot of minutes before it hove into our very relieved sight and we were able to get dressed and warm again. The driver had thought he would use his waiting time to go and fill up with petrol. Unfortunately for him - and for us swimmers - he had a puncture on the way, hence the delay. No one was any the worse for the experience but it was a lesson to me that when a notice says. 'Swimming Forbidden', it is probably very unwise to swim.

The Golan Heights and Caesarea Philippi

Since the Six Days' War of 1967 and the consequent taking over by Israel of those extensive areas of the Golan Heights which had previously been occupied by Syria, the strife and tension which have rarely been absent from the Holy Land during these years have often been linked with the Golan Heights in the minds of people in other countries. Accordingly, to those who have never been there, the prospect of actually visiting the Golan may seem a rather daunting, not to say frightening, one. The fact is, however, that it is a pretty straightforward and perfectly safe operation. It is a regular part of our Holy Land tour and I have been there year after year with my groups without ever having any untoward incidents.

Travelling north from Tiberias and taking the Capernaum road, we continue beyond Capernaum into what was Syrian territory before 1967 and find ourselves on a completely new road, built since the Six Days' War. Very soon it brings us to a bridge which carries us across the River Jordan close to the point where it flows into the Sea of Galilee. From here on the road rises steadily as we journey north and east for we are now on the lower slopes of the Golan range; and before long we are passing through territory that was the scene of battle in both the 1967 and 1973 wars. I remember one year having an Israeli driver who remarked to me in a matter-of-fact tone, as I sat next to him in the guide's seat, 'It was just here that we turned the Syrian advance in 1973. This was the furthest point they reached'.

By now well and truly on the Golan Heights, we see frequent evidence of past battles and of present military occupation. The road continues to climb until, after a while, we catch sight of Mount Hermon in the distance and shortly afterwards what is left of Kuneitra comes into view very close at hand. Before the Six Days' War, this was the largest town in the area and the headquarters of the Syrian army. It was left empty and desolate after the war and has now been mostly demolished. It stands just on the Syrian side of the present border with Israel and close to the United Nations settlement which oversees the business of keeping the peace. We are usually able to visit the United Nations military post at the Israeli end of the no-man's-land stretch of road between Israel and Syria. The one or two soldiers maintaining their often lonely vigil there are usually more than pleased to have some conversation to relieve their boredom.

Here, high up on the Golan plateau, we are very close to Mount Hermon which is never entirely free from snow and shortly afterwards we move on to the slopes of the mountain itself when we call at the Druze cafe at Birket Ram. Birket Ram means literally 'height pool' and the cafe, which sells luscious Druze sweet cakes along with its tea and coffee, is picturesquely situated beside a small lake in the crater of an extinct volcano. The upper reaches and majestic peaks of Hermon tower above the cafe and it is they that provide the winter snow slopes which afford skiing for many thousands every year.

The Caesarea Philippi of the New Testament is no more than seven miles, mostly downhill, from Birket Ram. On the way there we notice high above us the ruins of a Crusader fortress. Built to afford protection against possible Moslem attack from Damascus, it was known as Nimrod ('the hunter').

Today Caesarea Philippi is known as Banyas which is an Arabic corruption of the name Paneas, meaning a place dedicated to the god Pan. The reason for the corruption of the name is that the Arabs have no 'p' in their language; and the reason for the name is that the Greeks dedicated a shrine to Pan during their occupation here and named the place after him.

At a later stage in its history Tetrarch Philip renamed it Caesarea Philippi. This was in honour of the Roman Emperor with the addition of his own name to distinguish it from the Mediterranean port of the same name. This was its name in New Testament times but gradually it fell out of use to be replaced by Paneas, later Banyas, which is how it has been known ever since.

It is a ravishingly beautiful spot. Just to see it is to understand how, from time immemorial, people have felt it cast a spell of reverence over them. Its beauty is enhanced by the fact that the chief source of the River Jordan rises here and does so in spectacular fashion. It comes gushing out of the cliff face in front of the parking area already a full-blown river and soon to join with two other young rivers to form the Jordan.

For the Christian pilgrim, of course, the attractiveness of Caesarea Philippi rests chiefly not on its natural charm nor on its cradling of the infant Jordan River but on the fact that it was here that St. Peter first put into words the as yet only half-formed belief of the disciples that Jesus was the Messiah. It is true that they did not at the time fully understand but when I read the story

The Golan Heights and Caesarea Philippi

to my group in the shade of a tree at Caesarea Philippi, we can imagine something of what it must have meant to Jesus to have such a declaration of loyalty in that place at that time.

It was at Banyas, I recall, that I made my so far solitary attempt to teach stragglers a salutary lesson. Not infrequently we have one or more members of the group who persistently turn up late for departure, keeping everyone back and risking jeopardising the day's programme. In this particular year I had a couple who had been at fault in this way time after time and everyone was heartily sick of their selfishness. I had planned to insert a quick unscheduled visit to the nearby Banyas waterfall after leaving Banyas itself since we had, I estimated, time to do so.

When the bad timekeeping couple again failed to join the bus at the appointed time and were still not in sight five minutes after it, I decided to go to the waterfall without them. I expected to be back in about thirty minutes but, since they would not know where we had gone nor that I would be returning, I hoped they might "get the message'. Unfortunately for my plan, the bus had travelled only one of the two miles it had to travel to take us to the waterfall when it broke down. The driver speedily diagnosed the trouble and assured us it was not serious but that it would take him an hour to fix it. That put paid to my plan for inserting a 'bonus' visit to the waterfall. It also changed the complexion of the punishment exercise I had imposed upon our two stragglers. It was one thing to leave them for half an hour to reflect on their misdeeds; it was quite another matter to abandon them for more than an hour.

Someone, therefore, had to walk that mile back to Banyas in the heat of the noonday sun to acquaint them of the position. No prizes are offered for guessing who that someone had to be!

From Caesarea Philippi our north Galilee excursion takes us across the head of the Hula Valley to the modern town of Kiryat-Shemona ('the town of the eight'). This short journey is full of interest. During it we cross over the other two sources of the Jordan - the rivers Dan and Hatsban - and we pass by Tel Dan, the site of that city which was the furthest north city of ancient Israel. (There was a proverbial saying 'from Dan to Beersheba' which indicated the entire length of the country, Beersheba being the city furthest south.)

Kiryat-Shemona is a young town and is situated only a handful of miles south of the Lebanese border. It was given its name in honour of the eight young people (six men and two women) who died in the defence of the nearby Jewish settlement of Tel-Hai against an Arab attack in 1920.

My most dramatic memory of Kiryat-Shemona is of the year when, after finding the town basking as peacefully as usual in the afternoon sun, as we passed through it, with not the slightest hint of tension or fear far less of violence or warfare, we read in the 'Jerusalem Post' that evening that a rocket shell had landed in the centre of Kiryat-Shemona the previous afternoon.

My most bizarre memory of it goes back to my very first Holy Land pilgrimage. We had had a longish tour round several sites on the east side of the Hula Valley and our leader deemed it wise to let us have 'comfort stop' in Kiryat-Shemona. So we parked the bus, disembarked and followed Tim's guidance to the public toilets underneath the bus station. As we all trooped down the stairs we were met at the foot by an attendant who, as he directed the ladies to one side and the men to the other, thrust two pieces of toilet paper into the hand of each, whether it was wanted or not.

After passing through Kiryat-Shemona the road south to Tiberias runs along the eastern side of the Hula Valley which is surely the finest example one could ever expect to see of the scriptural promise being fulfilled that the desert will blossom like the rose. The River Jordan as it flowed south created three bodies of water in what is known as the Jordan Rift, a mighty geological fault that splits the Holy Land along its entire length. The Sea of Galilee and the Dead Sea have already been referred to; and the third is Lake Hula, the smallest and the most northerly.

Before the State of Israel came into being in 1948, the Hula Valley was full of swamps and almost totally unproductive, But the Israelis have transformed it. The swamps have been drained, the size of the lake has been greatly reduced and where there were malaria and stagnation now there are beauty and fruitfulness.

About ten miles south of Kiryat-Shemona the road passes by both the modern town of Hazor and, not far from it, the Tel and partially excavated ruins of biblical Hazor, a city that is prominent in early Old Testament history. Half a dozen miles further on we come to Rosh-Pinna. It is of no special importance today, although it was an important police post during the British Mandate, but it has a lasting significance as being the first settlement in Galilee. It was established in 1882 and it was because it was the first that it was given its name. Rosh-Pinna means 'chief cornerstone' and the reference is to Psalm 118:22 which says, 'The stone which the builders rejected is become the chief cornerstone'.

Just a mile or two before we pass under the Mount of Beatitudes and rejoin the coast road that takes us on our last lap to Tiberias, we see a sign indicating that Chorazin is only a mile and a half away along a side road. If time allows and we follow that road, it is to find that today there are only several huddles of building stones made of the black volcanic basalt characteristic of the region. In Jesus' day a small town occupied the site.

The Golan Heights and Caesarea Philippi

It is a reminder in somewhat salutary fashion of how Jesus passed judgement on Chorazin in its heyday. 'How terrible it will be for you, Chorazin' (Matthew 11:21). It helps us all the more perhaps to fit into the perspective of eternity the many things we have seen and reflected on during our day's excursion.

Visits That Were Not Pilgrimages

In addition to my pilgrimage tours of the Holy Land, I have visited it on two other occasions. I would like to give them a mention.

The first of them was, in fact, my first ever visit to the Holy Land. It was one of the British India Educational Cruises on *M.V. Dunera* (of blessed memory to many). Some 900 secondary schoolchildren were on board of whom about a third were from Glasgow; and I had been invited to be the Church of Scotland cruise chaplain. We were to be berthed at Haifa for Christmas Eve and Christmas Day, with bus tours to Jerusalem and to Galilee respectively on these two days. Never having been in the Holy Land before, I was as excited at the prospect of being there for Christmas as any of the young people were.

We stole into Haifa through the night while most of us were sound asleep. I will never forget the indescribable feeling of excitement of waking early, rising to look through my porthole and seeing Haifa shining in the morning sunlight under the benevolent gaze of Mount Carmel; and feeling awed with the realisation that this was the Holy Land and it was Christmas Eve.

Our trip so far had not been without its disappointments. The train taking us from Glasgow to Dover had been very cold, the channel crossing had been rough, our rail journey across the Continent had been subjected to many delays, fog had held up our departure from Venice, we met rough weather in the Adriatic, we experienced heavy rain in Athens. But none of these annoyances mattered in the slightest now; for it was Christmastide and this was the Holy Land.

When it came time to disembark into the line of buses waiting on the quayside, the sun was still shining brightly from a blue sky but when we reached Jerusalem nearly three hours later, the heavens opened and the deluge did not cease. All day we squelched and queued, queued and squelched as our some 1200 tourists (in addition to the students there were about 300 adult passengers) attempted to see the same sights and visit the same places more or less at the same time.

The rain and the consequent discomfort and inconvenience did not detract much, if anything, from the sheer thrill so many of us felt at seeing places whose names we had known from childhood and were now seeing for the first time. This was, I believe, especially so of Bethlehem, even though we were unable to visit it but had to be content with viewing it from afar and having the Church of the Nativity pointed out in the distance. A poignancy was added to the thrill by virtue of the fact that in order to look towards the birthplace of the Prince of Peace we had of necessity to look at the same time across the guns of the Jordanian soldiers facing us in their defence posts close by.

All of this combined to make our Watchnight Christmas Eve service on board ship the intensely emotional occasion many of us found it.

The following day, Christmas Day, it was sunshine all the way as the buses drove us through Galilee - to Nazareth, Tiberias, Beatitudes, Capernaum - and as we sailed on the Sea of Galilee. I for one was in a fever of excitement as I saw places I had known about since my Sunday School days and now was actually seeing. I have seen them many times since and have got to know them well; but that was my first sight of them and there is always something special about that.

When we cast off from our quayside berth that night, many of us stood for a long time at the stern of the ship watching the lights of Haifa recede into the far distance; and we knew that the memories would recede much more slowly.

My other non-pilgrimage visit was of a totally different character. It took place in February 1981 and my reason for being in the Holy Land at that time was to see a football match. Scotland were to play Israel in a World Cup qualifying match in Tel Aviv on Wednesday 15th February and my good friend, Ian Skelly, took me out as his guest with the Scottish Football Association official party on Sunday 12th. This gave us two clear days before the match and we hired a car on each of these days so that I could guide Ian around some of the sites, along with five others in the party whom we invited to occupy the vacant taxi seats, three SFA councillors plus two well known media personalities, Ian St John and Hugh McIllvanney. They made up an interesting and colourful group, and most enjoyable company.

The weather on our first touring day, the Monday, was fair and I was able to show them quite a lot of the Old City of Jerusalem. They appeared to enjoy it thoroughly, even though it struck them somehow as hilariously incongruous that I should say as we made our way down the Mount of

Travels in the Holy Land

Olives, 'We must hurry, for Gethsemane closes at noon'. I am so used to the constant juxtaposition in the Holy Land of the sacred and the secular, the romantic and the mundane, but my companions seemed to find it funny that I should express myself as I did. So much so that my remark managed to get itself quoted in the sports pages of one of our national dailies the following day.

It was not anything like so funny to my mind as the snapshot I took in the afternoon at the Wailing Wall. Since it was very much the off season for tourists, there was hardly anyone there apart from a few Israeli soldiers saying their prayers - in the usual fashion, facing the wall and rocking back and forwards on their heels. But when I was in the process of taking a photograph of Ian St John beside the wall, two enormously large Scottish football fans appeared as if from nowhere and asked me if I would take a picture on their behalf of them standing one on either side of this famous former internationalist and current television celebrity. I obliged but when I saw their massive bulks leaning inwards on either side of Ian, I could not help wondering how little of him might be left if they happened to collapse on top of him.

I had arranged to take the party to the Panorama Hotel for lunch where I normally house my groups for the Jerusalem part of our pilgrimage; and this was fitted in between the Mount of Olives and the Wailing Wall visits. Our hosts fêted us, refused to let me pay and capped the proceedings by making a presentation to me of a Scottish Saltire to take to the match on the Wednesday.

The weather on the Tuesday when we made a mini-tour of Galilee was foul. One of the Israeli FA officials told us it was the heaviest day's rainfall Israel had had for thirty years. What made things worse was that it was accompanied by a high wind. In Nazareth the streets were awash. The water was several feet deep and our driver was fearful that his car would be overturned.

I was very disappointed that my friends were not seeing Galilee wearing anything like its best clothes so far as weather was concerned. But we persevered. We had thought we might turn tail after our lunch at the Scottish Hospice in Tiberias but when the rain eased during lunch, we decided to pursue my original plan of driving all round the lake. In the event, however, we went no further than Capernaum before calling it a day and heading back for Tel Aviv.

Up till this point the weather improvement had continued. Although the rain had never completely ceased, it had slackened to a mere drizzle by the time we left the car in the parking lot and made our way into the Capernaum compound. But we had no sooner got there than the deluge began again, even more tempestuously than before. No other person was in sight in the whole of the excavations complex, except for one solitary figure draped in a huge Lion Rampant flag, a tartan tammy on his head and a beaming smile on his face. Recognising a fellow-Scot over for the match as we were - shrewd detective work, don't you think? - we nevertheless did no more than shout our greetings to him before rushing pell-mell to the shelter of our car. It was only when we were well started on our return journey that we began to wonder, How did he get there? How was he travelling? Where were his companions, if any?

I have no doubt that, whatever the answers to these questions, he would have been in attendance at the Ramat Gan stadium the following day to see Scotland beat Israel 1-0. We were there, too, and the result sped us on our homeward flight in a happy frame of mind. But our two days of touring left happy memories also. So far as I know, none of my companions had been in the Holy Land before and two days did not permit us to see all that much. Despite that, every time I meet any of them, he is sure to refer to those days with obvious pleasure. That perhaps illustrates how the Holy Land is likely to weave a kind of magical spell round nearly everyone who visits it, whatever the reason for the visit may be.

Difficulties of Communication

Communication difficulties are to be met in every realm of human life nor are they absent from the business of leading Holy Land pilgrimages.

The problem of communication is sometimes verbal. There is a story - apocryphal, I have no doubt, but I will repeat it just the same - of an officebearers' meeting in a Scottish church which illustrates the point. The recently installed minister of the church had become concerned about the level of the lighting in the sanctuary. During evening service in the winter, the illumination provided was in his opinion much less than satisfactory. Accordingly, at one of the monthly meetings of his officebearers he proposed that a chandelier should be acquired for the church. At once one of the older officebearers rose to his feet to object.

'I'm against getting a chandelier for the church', he thundered, 'and for three reasons. For one thing, I can't spell it. For another thing, I don't think anyone in the church will be able to play it. And for a third thing, what we really need in the church is something to improve the lighting'.

It is a fact, as so many know to their cost, that the problem of communication is universal; and every place and every sphere have communication problems peculiar to themselves. If you find it surprising that I should say that leaders of Holy Land pilgrimages encounter them, too, in the exercise of their leadership, I can only assure you that it is true.

Here also problems sometimes arise with regard to the spoken or written word. At times it may be because his pilgrim flock have not been listening as carefully as he imagined to the leader's assiduously prepared, immaculately enunciated and extremely important instructions. Like, for example, when he says, the night before a certain excursion, 'Be in the bus not later than eight o'clock tomorrow morning for that is when it will depart'; and then someone breezes along at ten minutes after eight, with the leader trying to

164

maintain a calm exterior and all the others saying to themselves, 'I could have had that other cup of coffee after all', and says airily, 'Oh, am I late? I thought we were to leave at quarter past'.

There was an occasion in our first Holy Land tour when my wife and I were the sufferers when verbal communication was somehow found wanting. On our first evening in Jerusalem, Tim Manson, our leader, proposed that those who felt energetic enough might like to go with him to visit the Garden of Gethsemane by night as a prelude to the planned itinerary due to begin the following day. Receiving a general murmur of interest and approval, Tim announced that he would arrange for taxis to transport us from the hotel. 'We'll not take names but those who wish to go should be in the foyer at 8.25 for a start at 8.30'.

We were very eager to be part of this extra expedition and, just to be on the safe side, we presented ourselves in the foyer at 8.15. A few were already there, one of whom said, 'I've looked outside. It's turned a bit chilly. Perhaps you should put on something warmer.'

'Have we time to go back to our room for that?', I asked somewhat apprehensively.

'Oh, yes', he assured us, 'In any case I'll tell Tim you are coming and we won't leave you behind.

But they did. We dashed upstairs to our bedroom, hurriedly donned pullover and cardigan respectively and dashed back down again, arriving in the foyer on the stroke of 8.30 to find it deserted. The Gethsemane party had already gone. Inexplicably Tim had not received the message that we were joining the trip and so we missed out on it. Being our first night ever in Jerusalem, we had not the foggiest idea of where the Garden of Gethsemane might lie and were too fearful of going in pursuit in case we should never meet up with our group.

That was a disappointment to us but there are times when the breakdown of verbal communication can be a source of embarrassment. On one occasion a misunderstanding over words led to a rather uncomfortable confrontation between one member of the group and myself. On the printed itinerary of which I had issued a copy to every member of the party, against a certain afternoon of our Jerusalem stay were set these words: 'Free afternoon. (Optional excursion to New City).' At our post-dinner meeting a day or two in advance of the free afternoon, I brought up the New City tour as one of the items of administration that required attention.

'You will be aware that Tuesday afternoon is free. You may either do your own thing that day or you may wish to accompany me on a bus tour of the New City, including visits to the Shrine of the Book, Yad Vashem, and the Holy Land Model. The cost of the tour will be £8 each. Please let me know

Travels in the Holy Land

how many of you wish to take the tour so that I may proceed to make the necessary arrangements.'

Before I could begin to take names and numbers, my clerical friend, for he was a retired minister, raised his voice, 'Wait a minute', he cried 'It says on the itinerary that Tuesday afternoon is *free*. Why are you now asking us to pay for it?'.

I strove as valiantly as the shock permitted but my striving was, I am afraid, unsuccessful in persuading him that 'free' in this context meant no more than freedom from a prescribed programme, freedom to choose how to spend the afternoon without missing out on any part of the included touring but not freedom from meeting the cost of the bus tour if that was one's preference. The optional New City tour went ahead and most of the group went on it - but not my protesting friend and his wife. Smarting under a continuing sense of injustice, he refused to participate in what he clearly saw as a bit of sharp practice by the tour company (or the leader?).

I fully expected him to register an official complaint with the company on his return but so far as I know he never did. Perhaps on reflection or a rereading of the itinerary wording he came to see the matter in a different light.

There was one tour, however, where a complaint was made against me as the tour leader on the basis of a not dissimilar misunderstanding of the brochure text. In the earlier days of my tour leadership the excursion from Tiberias to the Golan Heights and Caesarea Philippi was not, as now, part of the basic itinerary but was offered as an optional extra. When I offered it to the group, they seemed unanimous in their enthusiasm for it and all of them paid up their £10 for the whole day trip without either demur or pain.

Some two weeks after the pilgrimage was completed and we had all returned home, the tour company office informed me that one of my pilgrims had lodged a complaint to the effect that I had wrongly exacted payment from him for an excursion which was included in the basic itinerary for which, of course, payment had already been made as it was included in the tour cost. The man submitting the complaint was one with whom I had had a specially cordial relationship all during the tour. He was travelling on his own and had committed himself to delivering several talks about the tour upon his return home, and I had been trying to give him as much help as possible towards this end. I was quite thunderstruck to discover that he was claiming a refund of £10 on the grounds that on his return home he had reread the brochure and found that the 'trip to Caesarea was already included and Mr Martin was therefore in error in making a further charge for it'.

It was a pity he had not reread the brochure while we were still out there.

166

Difficulties of Communication

It would have been such a simple matter (I hope) to point out to him that while the already paid for itinerary included 'Caesarea', the optional (extra) excursion was to 'Caesarea Philippi', a quite different place. It was even more of a pity that he did not seem to recall having been to Caesarea (on the Mediterranean coast) prior to visiting Caesarea Philippi (on the Golan Heights). That would surely have oiled the creaking wheels of communication on this particular point.

Communication is not, of course, limited to the verbal vehicle. Sometimes - frequently, indeed - communication by visual means can be much more effective than mere words. Let me quote another apocryphal tale.

A long-distance lorry driver was sitting in a transport cafe eating his breakfast when half a dozen skinhead motorcyclists came noisily in and proceeded to give him a rough time. They shouted insults at him and when he made no reponse, they poured salt in his coffee and smeared the yoke of his fried egg on his hair. Still he uttered not a single word. Without speaking he rose from the table, paid his bill and walked out. 'What a lily-livered specimen that one is', the leader of the skinheads said to the waitress, 'Putting up with what we did and never one word of protest. He's just a coward.' 'Yes', replied the waitress, looking through the window to the parking area, 'And I'll tell you something else. He's a terrible driver as well. He's just driven his truck over six motor bikes.'

Visual communication can be very effective but it, too, can have its problems. It does not always work and even in the Holy Land it may fail to convey the right message. For even on Christian pilgrimage there are times and places where the visual aids of the sacred sites do not make the impact that might be expected. Many of them speak eloquently to Christian pilgrims of the life and message of Jesus but not all of them speak to everyone with the same clarity, not at first sight anyway.

It is not always easy, yet sometimes it is, as, for instance, when we are doing the Palm Sunday Walk or standing in the Garden of Gethsemane or sailing on the Sea of Galilee. There are times and places where invariably the visual communication spells out its message very clearly; but there are others where it requires a measure of conscious effort. That is why I often urge my groups in terms similar to those I employed to John in the Church of the Holy Sepulchre. This I do even in the Church of the Nativity which most people find eloquent in itself. I tell them that the church is very probably built over or very close to the actual place where Jesus was born; but I go on to stress that, nevertheless, that fact does not really matter all that much. What really does matter is the certain fact of Jesus' birth and the Church of the Nativity is a visible and memorable symbol of that. It is not what we are physically looking at that is of supreme importance; it is what is signified by what we see. It is the holy thing behind the holy place, that is what matters.

A basic problem of communication is that people may hear the same words and see the same scenes and yet have different perceptions of them. Just as some people will regard a church as half full while others will regard the same church as half empty, so people may hear or see the same things in different ways - and often do. This is at least partly the explanation of the intense disagreement between Arabs and Jews about their rights of occupation and possession in the Holy Land. Both of them quite sincerely regard it as their land and can adduce evidence for so doing. It is somewhat reminiscent, perhaps, of the old fable of the two brothers who came to blows because they disagreed about the nature of the shield which was suspended on a pole between them. One brother said it was gold, the other insisted it was silver. Neither would give way in his opinion and in the end a battle ensued with considerable damage to both. The sad thing was that both were right. The shield was gold on one side and silver on the other.

If only they had each tried to look at the situation from the other one's point of view, how much different the issue might have been. I do not offer any answers to the questions that divide Arab and Jew so tragically in the Holy Land today but as one who over the years has made many friends among both races, I grieve for the divisions that are causing so much suffering. When we are there on pilgrimage, we meet in the Holy Land many Israelis and we meet many Arabs, among them Jews, Moslems and Christians. Every night in our group meeting we pray for the people we have met and for the peace of the land; and after we return home, we continue to hope and pray that a new state of harmony or, at least, a strife-free working compromise may be achieved. I know that many people on both sides of the racial fence desperately long for such a solution.

To Be or Not to Be a Pilgrim

Whether or not it has shown through in these pages, I do not try to make any secret of the fact that so far as Holy Land pilgrimaging is concerned, I am an enthusiast. I cannot think of anything that could possibly be more exciting or more enriching for the Christian than to visit the land which saw Jesus born, saw him growing, working and teaching, and then saw him killed and resurrected from the dead. I can recall still, almost as if it was yesterday, the intense emotion that gripped me, a quarter of a century ago, when we disembarked from the aircraft at Tel Aviv for the very first time. When we had descended the aircraft steps and stood on the tarmac, I could not help saying to myself, 'Do you realise where you are? You have actually placed your feet on the very same country that was Jesus' home on earth'.

Sentimental, you might say. Naively romantic. Perhaps so but something of that same feeling seizes me every time I go back; and it intensifies as we go round the places Jesus knew and that knew him. To be able to sing in one's heart, 'I walked today where Jesus walked' is to sing a truly marvellous song.

Not everyone, I know, shares my enthusiasm. Some people are not even in favour of Holy Land pilgrimages at all. Most of these people, it is true, have never experienced a Holy Land pilgrimage personally. All the same they have a point of view that deserves to be respected.

Some are opposed in principle to the whole concept of pilgrimage in the modern world. They believe, sometimes very strongly, that it is a practice neither to be followed not commended. There is a real danger, they contend, that the pilgrim may be induced to worship shrines and locations instead of the God of whom these things purport to speak. I once had a friendly argument on this very point with a Moderator of the General Assembly of the Church of Scotland. 'I am not in favour of pilgrimages to the Holy Land', he asserted, 'Pilgrimage is an out of date conception. Trekking round the Holy Land paying homage to sticks and stones and memories of past days is an unhealthy practice. That sort of thing belongs to the Middle Ages and should not be encouraged in modern times.'

Modern Holy Land pilgrimaging would not dispute that 'that sort of thing' belongs to the Middle Ages and ought to be left there. It is true that that is how pilgrimages tended to be in the Middle Ages, usually a matter of reverencing a series of relics, often of doubtful authenticity, and as a result, more often than not, failing to see the wood for the trees. What modern Holy Land pilgrimages, properly conducted, seek to do is not in the least to induce worship of the holy places but to seek to help people see the holy thing behind the holy place and try to put it in the context of the present day and of people of the present day.

Some are opposed to the idea of a Holy Land pilgrimage so far as they themselves are concerned. They may have no objection to the principle of such a thing nor to others going on pilgrimage; but they are hostile to the notion of doing so themselves. It is not a simple matter of being disinterested. They are positively opposed to any suggestion that they should visit the Holy Land; and it is because they do not want to run the risk of having illusions shattered or preconceived ideas too rudely disturbed.

Professor William Barclay was like that. He was in the opinion of very many, myself included, the finest and most effective expositor of the New Testament of his time, especially to the non-academic man or woman. Although he died in 1978, his commentaries on the New Testament books (the world-famous Daily Study Bible) are still widely sold and read. But he never himself ever visited the Holy Land.

He and I were very good friends and I said to him one day, 'I'm surprised you've never been to the Holy Land to see the biblical sites for yourself. Wouldn't you like to go?'

He shook his head. 'No. I've never felt any wish to visit it and I have no desire to go now'.

'Why is that?' I persisted, 'Wouldn't it be good to see some of the places you've written about so much and so well?'

'That's just the point', he replied, 'I've formed my own clear mental pictures of the New Testament places and I'm perfect happy with them. I have no wish to run the risk of having these pictures destroyed or disturbed.'

Nothing I could say was ever able to change his mind in the slightest; and I have met quite a number of people who share his view, and take the same stance. They are afraid that actual sight of the Holy Land places might necessitate drastic revision of some of their mental images.

Indeed it might well have that effect but that is not, in my opinion, a good reason for not venturing to go and see things for oneself. My opinion derives not from the manner in which such a venture might rescue a writer like Willie Barclay from some plain, although relatively unimportant, errors of geography or topography. When, in the early seventies, I revised for him his seventeen volumes of the Daily Study Bible, I came across a few such errors which one visit to the Holy Land would have corrected for him.

Even more I have in mind the overall impact. It can not be denied that the first-time Christian visitor to the Holy Land is likely to encounter a visual shock or two as he is guided round the sites. Some long held and perhaps long cherished ideas of how this or that looked in Jesus' day may be rudely upset when the present reality comes into view, and not a little drastic readjustment may have to be made. But he or she will undoubtedly, I believe, emerge from the experience not only with a more accurate knowledge of what things look like now but also with a better grasp of what they probably looked like then; and, above all, a deeper understanding of their abiding message.

That, at least, has been my own experience; and it has, I think, been paralleled by the experience of all who have gone on pilgrimage with me and, I do not doubt, also by the experience of nearly all who have made a Holy Land pilgrimage. That has been the clear impression given me by any and all with whom I have discussed it; and that not only when they were still in the Holy Land but even long after they were back home and so, as it were, descended from the mountaintop to the plain. As a matter of fact, I have never come across any man or woman who has regretted making a pilgrimage to the Holy Land. In most cases their enthusiasm can scarcely be contained.

Strangely enough, the reaction of those who accompany a Holy Land pilgrimage while professing little or no religion is often one of warm appreciation. The vast majority of people who go on a Christian pilgrimage sort of Holy Land tour are likely to be committed Christians and churchgoers. But not all. Time and again I have had people approach me rather apologetically to explain that while they want to join one of my Holy Land tours (perhaps to accompany their spouse) they themselves are not really interested in the religious aspect of the tour and hope that I will understand. Of course I do and I am always happy to have such people come if they for their part are happy to be part of the group. In the event all of these have told me afterwards that they actually enjoyed the experience and not a few have confessed that to their surprise they were considerably impressed by the - from their point of view rather unwanted - 'religious aspect'.

A large number of people, of course, visit Israel for non-religious reasons.

Travels in the Holy Land

Many choose it simply as a country in which to spend a holiday. Eilat on the Red Sea is possibly Israel's best-known and most exotic holiday resort; and there is no doubt that it well repays a visit even for the single day which we at times manage to fit in as an optional extra. My own most abiding memory of visiting Eilat is not the cruise round the bay which lets us view through the glass bottom of the boat the marvellous coral formations and the myriads of brightly coloured fish of all shapes and sizes. It is not the stupendous underwater aquarium of modern vintage. It is not the eerie thrill of swimming off shore with the strange feeling of being only a few strokes away from the ships lying at anchor off the port of Aqaba in the country of Jordan whose border is so close. My most vivid memory is of the year when, on our return drive to Jerusalem, we happened to reach the southern extremity of the Dead Sea just as the sun began to set and daylight began to fade. As we drove northwards that day, the changing colours enfolding the hills on the other side of the sea, the hills of Moab, presented a scene of such beauty as is well beyond my capacity to describe with anything approaching adequacy. But I can tell you that I found it even more breathtaking than the fantastic display presented by the rock city of Petra. What we were privileged to see that day was a fascinating kaleidoscope of colour such as I for one had never seen before. Nor have I seen anything to match it since, even though I have been back to Eilat more than once. We must have been singularly fortunate that day to be in the right place at the right time. With the swift fading of light in the Middle East, the right time does not endure for very long.

That wonderful scene we were privileged to gaze upon across the waters of the Dead Sea would make a trip to Israel well worthwhile of itself for many a traveller. It is my conviction that it is even more worthwhile for the Christian traveller to walk where Jesus walked. Yes, I am an advocate of pilgrimages to the Holy Land in this twentieth century.

It's a Holiday as Well

I hope that what I have said in this book has not obscured the fact that a Holy Land pilgrimage is a holiday as well. It offers plenty of variety, lots of sunshine and a great deal of fun, all of which are recognised ingredients of the kind of holiday the average westerner wants. Mark you, it does not offer much in the way of another ingredient that many holidaymakers desire - namely, rest.

Most Holy Land tour leaders are likely to give clear warning to intending fellow travellers that if it is a restful holiday they are after, they are looking in the wrong direction. We proceed on the assumption that those who sign up for a Holy Land pilgrimage have the desire to see as much as is possible in the limited time available. As a result the itinerary is planned with the purpose of including as much as can reasonably be pressed into that time. In consequence the touring day will usually start around eight o'clock in the morning. Since it gets dark in the Holy Land in the region of six o'clock, summer and winter, unless artificial summer-time is introduced to extend the hours of afternoon daylight, it is imperative to make an early beginning to a sightseeing day and to keep at it fairly steadily once begun.

If, then, a leisurely two weeks' holiday is desired, a Holy Land pilgrimage is not likely to rank high on the list of possibilities. Such a pilgrimage is, however, meant to be enjoyed. It is not merely a 'do-goody' chore and certainly is not a penance. Far from being an activity of continuous and unrelieved dull piety, it has lots of fun attached to it.

The fun parts are often built into the plan. Just as often they are incidental happenings. Sometimes they are accidental. On occasion they may have an element of frustration, or poignancy. At times they may come to be fully appreciated only in retrospect. But they undoubtedly form a real and important part of any and every Holy Land pilgrimage. It may well be that some have been deterred from tackling a tour of the Holy Land because they do not realise this, just as people often miss out in other spheres on something worthwhile because they have no realisation of just what it is they are missing.

I had an experience of this nature on my first visit to the Holy Land. On a free afternoon in Galilee an optional tour to Mount Tabor was on offer but, among others, I declined because we counted it preferable to spend the afternoon lazing on the sun-drenched beach with an occasional dip in the sea. It was only after I visited Mount Tabor on my next tour that I discovered just what it was that I had denied myself.

There are times, on the other hand, where it is a considerable benefit to know the nature of what is being offered so that one may have the good sense to avoid it. There was, for instance, my first visit to Cana in Galilee and the church that stands there over the traditional site of the wedding reception at which Jesus changed water into wine to save loss of face for the hostess. After we had been round the church and concluded our brief devotions, the young curate who was temporarily in charge that day said, 'Perhaps you would like to purchase some wine made here at the church of the wedding feast? It was, of course, water this morning. Please let me give you a sample glass.' That act of generosity (whether or not approved by his parish priest, I do not know) was his undoing so far as sales were concerned. The wine tasted awful.

Holy Land pilgrims, I discovered at an early stage in my leadership experience, are not always sure of what is being offered to their view at any given time, even when they have seen it several times before. There are so many places of interest and so many experiences to share that it can, and often is, quite confusing to a 'first-timer'. One morning, on our fourth day in Jerusalem on a certain pilgrimage, as our bus passed by the Garden of Gethsemane which we had already visited twice and driven past more than once, one of my group said to me, 'Is this Bethlehem we are in now?' We had, in fact, already visited Bethlehem, too, but I was full of sympathy for the dear lady's confusion. I remembered much too clearly my own great difficulty on my first visit in attempting to unravel the seemingly hopeless entanglement of a mass of significant places seen in a short space of time.

It was confusion of a different kind that reigned in a broadcasting studio one morning shortly after one of our tours. Radio Clyde was presenting a programme that looked back on the pilgrimage and for that purpose had me in to chair a conversation about it with four of the group. In the course of this each of the four was to asked to describe what he or she had found to be the highlight of the tour for them. The programme was deliberately unscripted, for the sake of spontaneity, but was 'live', which made it all the more important that each of the four should know clearly the line that was to be followed. In particular we discussed beforehand what each was going to select as the highlight, since it was obviously undesirable that any two should choose to speak on the same location or event. Sorting this out proved none too easy but in the end agreement was reached. Bessie Park, for instance, was to speak about the Garden of Gethsemane and Jean Anderson on the Mount of Beatitudes.

On this basis we had a rehearsal, during which all went reasonably well and each of the four spoke fluently and to the point about their respective 'highlights'. In the beginning the actual broadcast went even better, and as I started, in the climax of the programme, to invite each to describe what they had found personally most memorable, the usual fears of potential disaster attending a live broadcast had been virtually laid to rest in my mind - but I was premature with my complacency. The first two highlights came and went very satisfactorily; but suddenly there was catastrophe when I turned to Bessie with Jean waiting come in fourth.

'It's your turn now, Bessie,' I said, 'Tell us what for you was the most memorable part of the tour.'

Without a moment's hesitation and with unbounded enthusiasm she said, 'Oh, without any doubt it was the Mount of Beatitudes and the wonderful open-air Communion service we had there overlooking the Sea of Galilee'. And on she went to give a vivid word picture of the scene and of the event. My face was probably a study. Jean Anderson's certainly was and as I faced her across the studio table, I could do no more than mouth silently to her, 'I'm sorry but you'll have to speak about something else. Just do your best'.

When Bessie finished and I invited Jean to describe her highlight, I was painfully aware that I was landing her with a very formidable task. I need not have worried. She rose to the occasion superbly and proceeded to speak about the Garden of Gethsemane with such fluency that no one would have suspected it was not her chosen and prepared subject. The producer was highly delighted with the end product while Bessie never, apparently, had the slightest idea that she had somewhat upset the applecart.

The consternation that Bessie caused me in that broadcasting station was of a totally different character from the consternation I felt early one morning - half past two, to be precise - when abed in the Panorama Hotel on the Jericho Road in Arab East Jerusalem.

I was wakened out of a deep (and no doubt much needed) sleep by an enormous clanging noise. It seemed to my ears for all the world like the sound of two metal dustbin lids being smacked together with great force and it was accompanied by a continuous loud shouting. Shaking the sleep from my eyes as best I could, I jumped out of bed and dashed to the bedroom window overlooking the street. I had little difficulty even in the darkness locating the culprit, the volume of noise he was creating making his position unmissable. I could make him out sufficiently in the dim light to see that he was armed with something not at all unlike the dustbin lids I had had in mind. Some sort of flat metal gong it was and he also had a thick stick with which he was hammering on his gong, only desisting temporarily every now and again to beat on every door he came to but never ceasing from his raucous bellowing.

Moslems are forbidden by their religion to drink alcohol and devout Moslems adhere to that prohibition. But I had long discovered that not every Moslem is devout and that not a few like to indulge a bit in alcoholic beverages. This, I thought, was such a one homeward bound from a late-night party and determined that everyone should be brought to wakefulness in order to share in his jollity. He was creating such a din that sleep was impossible, but before I could decide on any action that might be taken to get him quietened, he had passed by the hotel and gone on his way down the hillside into the village of Silwan, leaving no door unbeaten as he went.

In the morning I learned that I had sorely misjudged the nocturnal disturber of the peace. Far from being an irresponsible drunk, he was engaged on a religious mission, that of informing his fellow Moslems that the holy month of Ramadan was about to begin and summoning them to prepare for it. Ramadan is the thirty days' long annual religious festival of the Moslems which calls not only for special prayers but also for fasting and self-denial. From sunrise to sunset during these thirty days Moslems are forbidden to eat or drink or have sexual relations. My noisy friend's task was to make sure every one was awake in time to have a good meal before the first day of Ramadan dawned and then go for prayers to the mosque just across the Jericho Road from the hotel. Incidentally, I for one had just dropped off to sleep again after the Ramadan herald had been and gone when I was once more jolted awake, this time by the voice of the *muezzin* reverberating from the loudspeakers atop of the mosque as he called the faithful to prayer.

Exasperating as it might have been at the time, once we knew the real explanation of the commotion, most of us were pleased to have had the experience. It was another strand to be added to the varied texture of our Holy Land tapestry.

There was another occasion during a Panorama stay when the local colour provided had a grimmer aspect. The *intifada* was in being by this time and one evening the hotel shop failed to open. It was manned by the hotel photographer who the previous morning had taken a photograph of all the group on the flat roof of the hotel with the Old City of Jerusalem as background; and he was supposed to have the photographs ready for us that evening. When I enquired about his absence, I was informed that he was in gaol, having been arrested by an Israeli army patrol.

He appeared back in the hotel, with the photographs, the next evening and told us what had happened. He had gone to collect our developed and printed photographs and was making his way back to the hotel, carrying the photographs in a satchel, when a passing army jeep descended upon him and took him into custody for 'being in possession of a suspicious parcel'. Under the circumstances I refrained from enquiring as to whether their verdict of 'suspicious' had been arrived at before or after they had inspected our photographs.

When staying in the Panorama Hotel with the densely populated village of Silwan sprawling down the hillside below us, we were never in any grave danger of over-sleeping, even outwith Ramadan and the *intifada* and apart from the prayer calls from the adjacent mosque. Early in the morning a cock is sure to crow and a donkey will start to bray. I do not suppose they have been the same cock and the same donkey all down the years, but they sound the same and they have the same effect of helping us to rise early and make the most of the new day.

We had a driver once who was not prepared to depend on any other kind of early morning alarm system on the morning of our departure from Jerusalem save a personal telephone call from the group leader. It was the year we were staying in St Andrew's Hospice over St Andrewstide, and we were to leave there at six o'clock in order to catch the Heathrow flight from Ben Gurion. The driver needed to have his bus at the hospice by 5.30 in order to load first the baggage and then the passengers. We were to rise at 5.15 for a quick breakfast before departure. At the close of the previous day's touring the driver said to me, 'I'm a very heavy sleeper and a poor riser. You will need to telephone me at four o'clock in the morning to make sure I am awake and you must keep ringing until I answer'. And so it was that while the remainder of the group were blissfully turning over to enjoy the last delicious hour and a quarter of their slumber, their devoted but very envious leader was dragging himself out of bed to creep downstairs in the dark and cold of the December morning to the public telephone in order to ensure that the party got to the airport in time. My being required to alarm call the driver was unexpected as well as unwelcome.

Another unexpected and unwelcome circumstance befell us the time we were in Israel for Scotland's World Cup match against the home country - in February 1981. The SFA party arrived at Ramat Gan stadium in Tel Aviv after a morning of heavy rain to find pools of water everywhere on the approach to the ground on a cold, overcast afternoon. A number of the party thought it prudent on such a day to seek a 'comfort stop' prior to settling down on the stone seats (designed for the usual warm weather?) for the next two hours.

Travels in the Holy Land

On enquiring of an attendant where the toilets were located, they were thrown into some consternation when he replied, with no demonstration of concern, 'The toilets are locked'.

'How about opening them now, then?' was the anguished cry.

'I'm not able to open them', came his reply in the same matter-of-fact, unconcerned tones, 'The man with the keys hasn't turned up.'

What a scenario for a Whitehall farce! A World Cup football match and a mere thirty minutes before kick-off time the only man with keys to open up the toilets had not turned up. Nor did he ever turn up. And no one else was either able or willing to do anything about getting the toilets opened. A veil will now be discreetly drawn over the desperate measures that had to be taken that day by some desperate men caught in a desperate situation.

I had another experience on that trip - of a vastly different kind - which has not been forgotten and never will be. On the evening before the match Ian Skelly took me, along with Morag Park, one of my High Carntyne members then working in Israel, and Isobel Goodwin, the head teacher at Tabeetha School, out for dinner in Jaffa. After a lovely meal, Ian suggested that we look for a taxi to take us back to Tel Aviv where our hotel and their flat were both located. 'Let's walk', said Isobel, 'It's not much more than a mile and it is a pleasant walk along by the sea. I've done it many times. It will take us only about twenty minutes.'

And so we walked. But Isobel had not reckoned with the fierce wind that had sprung up and, heavily laden with sand, blew violently against us all the way. It was a real battle to make progress and it took us nearly an hour to cover that mile and a bit; and at the end of it our hair was so full of sand that it took a lot of shampooing to remove it.

It was not long after this that Isobel was plunged into the long fight against the cancer which eventually caused her death at the age of forty-two. I often recall that night of strenuous battle against the wind and I think it was not unlike the brave battle which Isobel was soon to wage against her illness. Except, some may say, that we did get to our destination in the end; but, then, so did she, I believe, just as I believe that for every Christian pilgrim, whatever the struggles, there is a happy journey's end.